LEADER
BY DESIGN

COLLEEN CALLANDER

WHAT PEOPLE SAY ABOUT COLLEEN CALLANDER

'Col has a natural power to mesmerise a room with her voice. She is a true visionary. She has always empowered me and given me the autonomy to realise my creative ideas. She taught me to be open and honest and gave me the confidence to express my ideas with passion and conviction.'

Kerrie Nelson, Director and Founder, Gypsy River and Gypsy River House

'Every now and again you meet and work with stand-out people. I'm talking about a great listener; an authentic, interested, laser-focused, clever, caring, giving (with a roll-up-your-sleeves and get-stuff-done attitude) person. That's Colleen.'

Lisa Kingman, Managing Director, Social Good

'Colleen is a dynamic, sophisticated and compassionate leader. Her tenacious and assertive approach in business is beautifully complemented by her attention to emotional detail, openness in communication, and appreciation of the essentiality of cultivating wellbeing in the corporate sphere. Colleen leads with elegance, generosity and grace.'

Meredith Gaston, author, artist, wellness coach and speaker

'As one of Australia's leading CEOs, and as a new ambassador for CEO Dare to Cure and the Children's Cancer Institute, Colleen has passionately engaged with our organisation. She has made a real and significant philanthropic impact and helped raise vital research funds to ultimately find a cure for every child.'

Cameron Bayfield, Corporate Partnerships Manager, Children's Cancer Institute

'When I met Colleen, I instantly felt connected to her spirit and likeable nature that oozes girl-next-door-meets-exciting-entrepreneur. What I love about Colleen is that she knows who she is and what she stands for. She's inspiring and grounded and makes you want to learn more and more from her.'

Amanda Campbell, sports kinesiologist, multiple sclerosis ambassador and mindset coach

'Colleen is a true leader for our times: generous and purpose-driven. She inspires women to truly believe in themselves, to give hard stuff a go and to use their voice to strive for bigger things. She is kind and empathetic and leads with integrity and purpose.'

Olivia Ruello, CEO, Business Chicks

'Colleen is one of the most influential and dynamic forces in the Australian fashion industry. Her unique ability to lead, have an impact and remain relevant in one of the most competitive industries is truly remarkable. She has empowered and led thousands of women over her dynamic career and is a phenomenal role model all women can learn from.'

Jess Thomas, Founder, Health Lab Australia

'I started my career as a young adult in my early 20s and Colleen quickly became my mentor, the leader I looked up to and an amazing role model – not only for me but also for everyone around her. Colleen was the kind of leader I wanted to be. Colleen challenged me, empowered me and taught me the importance of believing in myself and staying true to my values.'

Cristiana Bronson, National Sales Manager, Sportsgirl

'I have had the privilege of working with Colleen for many years as she has supported my charity. The kindness she has constantly shown has always stood out and made me feel welcome whenever I went to Sportsgirl. Her continuous support and generosity have been a cornerstone for our long relationship and I've always felt inspired after being in her presence.'

Melissa Azzopardi, National Partnerships Executive, Starlight Foundation

'Colleen is an exceptional leader and a once-in-a-lifetime boss. Working alongside Colleen as her EA, I was reminded daily of all the possibilities available to me simply because she supported, inspired and believed in me. Actually, this wasn't just a luxury afforded to her inner circle – she did this for all her team. I witnessed Colleen's unique leadership throughout the years. Truth be told, I could have worked anywhere but I chose to stay, as it's hard to accept the old way of business once you have been shown a new world of possibilities and been empowered to lead with kindness.'

Tennille Younger, former EA to the CEO, Sportsgirl

'A forever-personal-friend who demonstrates constant fierce loyalty, compassion and incredible drive. Colleen is a woman who can empower anyone to strive to find the best version of themselves. She is extremely zealous about family and life balance, and her can-do-will-do attitude to life is infectious. She inspires through confidence and inclusivity of all.'

Debbie Talbot, Director, AND Communications

First published in 2021 by Major Street Publishing Pty Ltd
PO Box 106, Highett, Vic. 3190
E info@majorstreet.com.au
W majorstreet.com.au
M +61 421 707 983

A catalogue record for this book is available from the National Library of Australia.

Printed book ISBN: 978-0-6489803-8-4
Ebook ISBN: 978-0-6489803-9-1

Cover design by Tess McCabe
Cover photograph by Susan Bradfield
Internal design by Production Works
Printed in Australia by Ovato, an Accredited ISO AS/NZS 14001:2004
Environmental Management System Printer.

10 9 8 7 6 5 4 3 2 1

One

THE DAY I (ALMOST) THREW IT ALL AWAY

Leadership is about
one life having an impact on
another in a positive way.

COLLEEN CALLANDER

$\mathcal{A}\delta$ women and especially mothers, we often put others before ourselves. It can be subconscious – a natural inclination. For me, this took its toll and came at a great cost.

I'm sure you've felt that cost in your life at one time or another. But have you ever reached the point where you decided you're done? Enough is enough? This is it?

That moment came for me in 2007. I was the general manager of Sportsgirl; my usual role was head of retail operations, but I was covering the general manager for her maternity leave. I was the proverbial headless chicken.

To say I was 'busy' is an understatement. With three children – Macey was just two, Trent was nine and Jake was 10 – an average day was barely contained chaos. Trent had been just nine months old when I joined Sportsgirl; I was still breastfeeding, pumping milk twice a day in the office, and taking all of my breast pumping equipment with me on planes.

As my role evolved, so too did my busy lifestyle. It involved everything from raising small children to having days packed with meetings, appointments and leadership decisions. My mum was my main support person – without her, I actually couldn't have done it. She did the school runs for me and I always attempted to leave work on time so I could be home for bath time, meal time and family time.

Then, after everyone was asleep and the house had quietened down, I'd start shift two. I'd pick up my computer and work for a couple more hours; it wouldn't be unusual to see me mopping floors and making school lunches at midnight.

That's if I wasn't travelling – my job saw me trek all over Australia for various reasons.

On the weekends, I'd take the kids to sports and activities and, between all of this, I tried to spend time with my husband, and vaguely stitch together a social life on the weekends.

Did I mention that I lived in Geelong while I was doing all of this? I was commuting 90 minutes each way per day to get to Melbourne for work. Is it any wonder that I was feeling burnt out?!

Perhaps this crazy schedule sounds familiar to you. For me, it was all I had ever known. For eight years, way back when my second child was still in nappies, I had worked my way up the corporate ladder at Sportsgirl – moving from state manager to national manager to retail operations manager, before taking the role of acting GM.

I sometimes think of myself during this period as a Formula 1 race car – one that had not been refuelled or serviced, had its tyres changed or pulled into the pit stop in a very long time. I was a high performer but, boy, I was suffering.

I had just been going and going and going. I knew no boundaries and said 'yes' to everything, no matter how full my plate. I wanted to be the perfect wife, mother, friend, sister and daughter. I put everyone else's needs before my own – and before my health.

No-one asked me to do all of this, mind you – it was just me. I have always been a people pleaser. My whole childhood was about pleasing my mum and dad and making them proud, and that flowed through to the way I lived my life. Making my boss proud... my kids proud... my husband proud... That's all that mattered to me.

Until I couldn't do it any longer.

THE TIPPING POINT

I was only 36 years old, but I was *utterly burnt out*.

I got home from work one night and as I walked through the door and saw my husband, the words tumbled out of my mouth. 'I can't do it anymore. I'm exhausted. I am burnt out – I'm done.'

This was very typical of my personality; I'm an 'all or nothing' kind of person, which is probably why I had reached burnout in the first place!

It's not that I had lost my passion – far from it. I absolutely loved my job and was so proud of what I'd been able to achieve in my career. I just didn't have anything left in the tank. I had hit a wall... any cliché you can think of, that's how I felt.

What I've come to learn in the years since is that my problem was a very common one among women.

I didn't realise it at the time, but I was totally neglecting myself and my own health in my quest to make everyone proud of me. I think this came from my mother; she was always a pleaser and put others' needs before her own. (She still does!)

So there I was, always the first to arrive and often the last to leave the office. (I was one of those people who thought the longer you worked the better – it showed commitment and drive. This was how I was brought up.)

I was also on a plane every second week and, because I wanted to be an inspiring leader, my door was always open for my team. In fact, I always put my team's needs before mine, too. Hence, my breaking point.

Back to that conversation with my husband.

'I'm done,' I repeated. 'I just don't want to do it anymore.'

I am so lucky that I have such a supportive husband. His immediate reply was, 'If you don't want to do it anymore, then don't. Nothing is worth your health.'

So, we sat there (me in a very emotional state) and discussed our plans. We could sell our home and move to our holiday house in Sorrento (we wouldn't be able to afford two homes), and take the boys out of private school and enrol them into the local public school. We would have to change our lifestyle, but it would be worth it to focus on my health and wellbeing and that of my family.

That's the thing about burnout or exhaustion; it doesn't just affect you, it affects everyone around you. You are tired, cranky, emotional and sometimes even irrational. Your loved ones don't get the best version of *you* when you're in this state.

Perhaps you have experienced burnout previously, are in the midst of it right now or are on the slippery slope towards it. I wish I knew then what I know now; I wish I'd known the signs that very quickly creep up on you when you're on that narrow, windy and bumpy road to burnout.

I also wish I'd understood the importance of self-care and self-preservation. This is why I want to share my experience and failures with you: because I'm passionate about helping other women recognise the signs of burnout before they reach the same dire point I did. I want to empower you to be comfortable with putting yourself first, and to live a life of self-care and self-love – because when we do this, we have so much more to give others.

After that emotional planning session with my husband I had a fitful night of sleep, and awoke the next day feeling exhausted and anxious – yet relieved. The relief was the most overpowering feeling, because for once, I felt like I was about to get off this train to Burnout Town.

As soon as I got to work, I made a beeline for my boss's office. I could barely get the words out fast enough.

'I am letting you know what I am resigning,' I said. 'I'm burnt out, exhausted and my health is suffering. I quit.'

Oh, sweet relief.

I knew that once I said it out loud I would feel like a huge sandbag had been lifted off my shoulders – and it did. I felt like I could *breathe* again.

For a moment, at least.

*Burnout is
a sign that
something needs
to change.*

SARAH FORGRAVE

A DOSE OF SELF KINDNESS

You see, my boss at the time didn't see this coming. He was shocked I wanted to walk, and didn't want to accept my resignation!

'Col, what can we do?' he said to me. 'We don't want you to resign. You are such an asset to the company. There has to be another way...'

As it turns out, I didn't end up walking out that day. Over the coming weeks, we sat down together and had lots of discussions about my unsustainable working hours, my lack of home/life boundaries and how utterly exhausted I was – again, all things I had put on myself.

'What will it take for you to feel refreshed and refuelled?' he asked. 'Eight weeks off? Ten weeks? We can work this out, we don't want you to leave.'

In the end, I took three and a half months off. I used that time to refuel my tank – I put the Formula 1 race car in for a well-overdue service of self-care and kindness.

Not only did I work on my emotional and physical wellbeing during this break, but I also knew I needed to make some significant changes in my life so that I would never end up back in that same place, ever again. This was the best lesson ever in self-care. Realising I couldn't help others unless I helped myself first was a total game changer.

It's not your job to like me, it's mine.

BYRON KATIE

I returned to the office in February 2008 after three and a half months of rest, recharging and support from a life coach. I had never felt better. With my tank now full and strategies in place to live my best life (without burnout!), I was ready to tackle anything.

When I look back on this period, I realise that if it wasn't for the kindness, empathy and strategic thinking of my bosses at the time, I might be living a very different life right now.

I would not have had the opportunity to work my way up the corporate ladder and, more importantly, I would not have been able to inspire, impact and influence so many people through my leadership journey.

My own experiences have shown me that we need to empower and inspire women to lead in their own lives – both at work and personally.

We need to create a world where we lead with kindness, humility and self-awareness – a world that puts *people* at the heart of everything we do.

All of which has led me to write this book. My goal is to inspire women to step up, have a voice, live with purpose, become the leaders they want to be, change the rules, live with confidence and create cultures that inspire and empower. I want them to embrace their superpowers. I also hope this book inspires organisations to embrace a new era of leadership – one based in kindness, trust and authenticity, and that encourages more women to take the helm.

step up

live with

purpose

change the rules

inspire &
empower

live with

confidence

speak up

embrace your
superpowers

A worldwide epidemic

Burnout costs billions of dollars every year in healthcare costs. It endangers the health of millions. It's perhaps no surprise to learn that burnout affects more women than men. Research shows that 23 per cent of employees feel burnout often, and 44 per cent feel burnout sometimes. Burnout often leads to disengaged employees, who cost their employers 34 per cent of their annual salary as a result. It's also responsible for a significant amount of employee turnover – between 20 and 50 per cent or more, depending on the organisation.

Signs of burnout show up in many different ways, and we need to recognise these warning bells before we get to a point where burnout takes over. Do any of these ring true for you?

- Chronic exhaustion
- Concentration and memory problems
- Constant fatigue
- Difficulty 'switching off'
- Inability to make decisions
- Irritability and lack of patience
- Lack of energy
- Reduced performance
- Sleep disorders or insomnia
- Trouble focusing on the task at hand

If you are nodding along as you read this, flick to chapter 7 *now!* It's where I share the strategies and solutions I personally used (and that I share with my mentoring clients) to get myself out of this funk.

A MISSION TO ENGAGE, EMPOWER AND INSPIRE

I eventually became the CEO of Sussan for six years, and then CEO of Sportsgirl for the next seven years, until I stepped out at the beginning of 2020. After 30 years in retail and an amazing 20 years with the Sussan Group, it was time for me to make a change and write the next chapter of my life.

I initially left to have a break and pursue my passion projects: supporting and mentoring women, writing this book, travelling and doing some charity work. Funnily enough, the break didn't actually happen – I've been so busy! But I've been busy in a *great* way: so many new doors have opened and I have so many exciting projects on the go.

As a CEO, my mission was to engage, empower, inspire and enable people to bring their best selves to work each day. Now, in this next chapter of my life, my mission is the same! I want to engage, empower and inspire as many people as I can, one beautiful human at a time.

As leaders, it's our job to create cultures that allow people to work at their natural best – and, in turn, help our organisations to grow and thrive.

We need to create a world of amazing female role models who embrace self-confidence and self-care. We need to foster humility, compassion and collaboration. We need to understand our core values in order to lead with authenticity, and create workplaces that align with these values.

This book is part autobiography – I share my life journey, including how my upbringing shaped the woman and leader I am today. But it's also packed with tips, advice, insights and guidance relevant to all women – whether you're climbing the corporate ladder, an entrepreneur, a volunteer, a professional athlete, working in the family business or holding down a casual job while raising a family.

Regardless of your current role and situation, I want to empower you to lead in your own life.

You don't build a business - you build people - and then people build the business.

ZIG ZIGLAR

We all need to play a part in this future world – and this is why we need to embrace female leadership. Only 17.1 per cent of CEO roles in Australia are held by women. This is a number that, in my view, is far too low.

Less than 20 per cent of CEO roles in Australia are held by women.

Growing up and in the early days of my career, I looked up to and admired people with titles, levels of authority, rank and positions of power, labelling them leaders. What I learnt over time in both life and business is that these trappings do not automatically qualify a person for leadership. Leaderships starts with the person. You don't even need a title to be a leader. Every day we have the ability to lead in our own lives, through every action, interaction, reaction and decision we make. We all have the ability to become the leader we always wanted to be, and the leader we always wanted to follow.

From a young age, I was always intrigued with the way people behaved, both good and bad. What made people treat others with kindness and respect? What made people step all over others for their own gain? What made some people create environments of fear, and others environments of collaboration? Why were some people caring and others cruel? Why were some generous and others greedy?

Looking back, I now know that I was shaping myself into the leader I wanted to be *by observation*. I listened, I learned, I asked questions and I made mental notes.

Without knowing it, I was becoming a **leader by design**.

We all have the ability to become a *leader by design* in business and in life.

PEOPLE BEFORE PROFIT

During my 13 years as CEO of two of Australia's most recognised women's fashion brands, I have led with purpose, stayed true to my values, inspired and empowered women to believe in themselves, encouraged and nurtured, and created a culture of care that has allowed people to shine.

It saddens me that in today's world the majority of people go to work each day uninspired! I want to change that by sharing both *why* and *how* organisations can change the way they lead – by embracing a new era of leadership, and by encouraging more female leaders to have the confidence to step up and have a voice.

Can you imagine a world where people get up every day feeling valued, inspired, empowered and fulfilled? In 2020, Gallup reported that only 34 per cent of people in the US (and only 15 per cent worldwide) are engaged with their jobs.

This is because so many organisations today play the short game – putting profits before people. Think mass lay-offs to balance the books, increased market value and shareholder returns, all focused on short-term gains.

What would happen if we changed the emphasis from **profit** to **people, purpose** and **passion**? To me, these characteristics are the foundations for creating organisations that will not only survive but also thrive.

People with purpose and passion = profit.

I am a leader who has played the long game – people before profit. That does not mean profit is not important; of course it is. I would not have been a successful CEO for many years if I thought running a profitable and sustainable business was not highly important. But I believe if you look after your people, the profits will follow.

As a leader, I have always focused on creating winning teams and environments where people felt inspired and empowered, and love to come to work. I nurtured a culture of care, developed and retained talent and inspired female leaders for the future.

I want this book to be an inspiration to women (as well as men) of all generations. I want to encourage women globally to believe in themselves and their abilities, share their voices, lead with kindness, take action and bring equality into boardrooms, organisations and communities – and even into their homes.

I want all women to believe in the power within. It is possible to become the leader you always wanted to have, and the leader you always wanted to be, in business and in life.

So let's get started!

Two

THE QUEEN OF
PEOPLE PLEASING

Don't be afraid
of losing people;
be afraid of losing
yourself by trying
to please everyone
around you.

HELEN BARRY

Before I go any further, I want to make it clear that I credit my parents for the success I have achieved as a woman and leader. I am so extremely grateful I received the best of both of them in my genes and habits. My business acumen comes from my dad; my caring and nurturing ways from my mum. My strong work ethic and intrinsic tendency to work hard came from both.

But I also learned, throughout my childhood, how to become an expert in pleasing people. This, I have since learned, almost always works out well for other people – but it doesn't go so wonderfully for the person doing all of the pleasing!

BUILDING THE FOUNDATIONS

I spent much of my childhood listening to and learning from my dad. He is Italian, and landed in Australia at age four with his mother, his brother, the clothes they wore, a few suitcases and a very small amount of savings. (They were meeting his father, who had immigrated earlier.) After finishing school at the age of 14, he became a concreter and bricklayer by day and worked at the abattoirs by night.

He was not even a man, barely a teenager, but he had already been thrust into an adult's world. He left school to start working full-time not because that was necessarily what he wanted to do, but because he needed to earn money so he could help support his family. He was an absolute workhorse – and still is today.

My mother had a very different upbringing. She was one of 12 children, had an alcoholic father and lost her own mother when she was just 21 years old. Not only did she have the job of looking after her own two babies – myself and my older brother – but she also took on a motherly role for her younger siblings. She was nurturing and caring and always put others' needs before her own.

Mum was the person I would go to when anything went wrong. Bloody knees from falling over, chasing my brother up the side lane of our house; mosquito bites all over me, even though I'd been told to put repellent on; or when I just needed a cuddle. I knew that she would make everything okay.

Over the years, I watched my dad and his family work their fingers to the bone to build the life that so many immigrants dreamed of. My dad and grandfather were both great with their hands, and given English was their second language, and not one that they were confident in, jobs such as concreting, bricklaying and building seemed like good options. My grandmother and uncle went to work on farms harvesting peas and potatoes. My dad and his family saved every penny they could. Between them, they purchased their family home and then a block of land, which they later built four units on.

A few years later, with the rental income from the units, they purchased another block of land and built another four units... and the story continued. Sadly, my grandparents and uncle are not alive to see the successful self-made property entrepreneur my father has become – but I know they would be very proud of him.

With my father involved in so many different aspects of business – including property development, building and small business ownership – conversations over dinner during my childhood often consisted of business talk. I was all ears.

Money, turnover, rent, investments, cost of goods, buying and selling... it was intoxicating. When people turned up for business meetings I would sit next to my dad like I was invisible, but I was listening in on every detail.

Dad was a tough negotiator. He taught me about hard work and how important money was. He would always say, 'Money doesn't come easy; you have to work hard for it.' He definitely instilled a strong work ethic in me and my siblings and, from as early as I can remember, I always loved to work.

At eight years of age, I was working weekends and school holidays in my parents' canteen at the local Geelong pool. I remember my mum and dad always saying to me, 'Col, go and have a swim. Take a break for a while.' My response was always the same: 'I'm fine; you both have a break and then I'll have mine.' I would work for hours and hours without a break – not because I had to, but because I wanted to.

It genuinely mattered to me that my parents were proud of me. At the time, I thought I was refusing breaks and working as much as I did so that I could be caring, polite, respectful – a good child. What I realise now is that I was always desperately wanting my parents to be proud of me. That pride came from being a hardworking and caring person. It was my way of getting feedback that I was 'doing good'. 'Others before self' became a lifelong habit that has stayed with me – often at great personal cost.

The days at the canteen were long, hot and very busy. I loved every minute of them! I loved working, I loved making a little bit of money… and I especially loved my parents being proud of me.

My final destination at the end of the day would be the oval marble coffee table in the middle of the lounge room. With my knees tucked under me and my tired little body melting into the blue and gold carpet, I was surrounded by bright green buckets overflowing with coins. I would count the coins out one by one into perfect piles, bagging them up all into their types. The one, two and five cent coins were my 'pay' for a long day's work.

My dad called me canteen manager by day and bank manager by night. He was not one to share his emotions or even openly give credit (this was not how he was brought up), but in these small gestures I felt Dad's pride in me – even though he didn't say the actual words.

From around 10 years of age, I would go to work with my father on building sites; any chance I got, I would ride alongside with him in his ute and head off to the day's adventure. I can still recall the excitement of waking up in the dark – because it was always a *very* early start – and setting off to the worksite with Dad, being allowed to sit in the front seat and coming home with him in the dark.

On site, I'd move bricks, stack branches and push the wheelbarrow around, picking up rubbish. Again, the days were long, and I worked hard. Whenever anyone would ask my father a question, he would say, 'You better check in with the boss,' gesturing towards the blonde, curly haired little kid in brown cord pants, a brown hand-knitted jumper and black gumboots, with a dirty face and all of 100 cm tall. Everyone laughed – but I loved it when he said that. I felt important and useful and I felt his pride in me.

My upbringing and this foundation of knowledge, discipline and nurturing contributed to my achievements, not least being my membership of the '20 per cent Club' – so named due to the dismal percentage of women in CEO positions in Australia.

MY SLIDING DOORS MOMENT

My road to leadership launched in earnest in the mid '80s.

The bell rang and the classroom erupted. Another school year had come to an end – Year 11 was *done!*

The sun was mid sky, beaming down with all of its intensity. The air was still and hot – a typical Melbourne December day.

Shrieks and screams filled the air as we all bustled out the school gates, excited that the summer holidays were finally here. Boys, beaches and fun in the sun were the key topics of conversation for my girlfriends. But not for me...

I was excited for a different reason. I had lined up my first summer job, and although I had always worked in the family businesses growing up, this was my first *real* job – and to top it all off, it was in the fashion industry.

Day one of my first proper job, as a summer casual at my local Just Jeans store in Geelong, could have been day one at Chanel. I was in absolute *heaven*. Unbeknown to me at the time, this would be the start of my 30-year retail career.

I loved it from the minute I walked onto the shop floor. I mean: *I loved it!*

I loved serving customers. I loved unpacking stock. I loved refolding the denim wall and I loved learning about the product, how to merchandise and how to use the computer. I strived for perfection – no matter what the task, I gave it my all.

I worked every shift I could get over that summer break. At the end of the holiday period, the area manager approached me and asked if I'd like to stay on and join the Just Jeans team full-time. She said that they were so thrilled with the job I had done over summer that they wanted me to stay – and that I had potential to progress through the company.

It was like being on that building site with Dad all over again. Being noticed for doing the most mundane jobs to the best of my ability, and with passion and care, had once again paid off.

I was ecstatic! I couldn't wait to get home and tell my parents.

All I could think about was how I'd been noticed, that I had 'potential' and that a summer casual job I had absolutely adored was about to turn into a long-term, proper job with real career prospects.

When I take myself back to that moment in time in my memory, I can still tap into the excitement. I remember that day so vividly.

It had been a super-hot day. Although it was now late afternoon, the heat of the sun was still intense. It was like running in a tumble dryer, but I ran all the way home, sucking in deep breaths as sweat poured from my brow and down my back. I had adrenaline coursing through my body and my face ached from smiling at the offer I had received.

I made it home in record time. I ran up the brown pebble steps to the front door... and, as I put the key in the lock, reality hit me.

I visualised what would be on the other side of the door: two parents who had worked incredibly hard to put me through school and who had great career aspirations for me upon finishing my senior school education. I was about to shatter all of their dreams by accepting a job in retail.

The thought of letting my parents down, merging with the excitement of the opportunity I had just been presented, which I so dearly wanted to grab with both hands – well, it was almost too much to bear. It was like an explosion of emotion.

My parents were the most important people in my life. I just wanted to make them proud. But I had a feeling this wouldn't make them very proud of me at all.

I took a deep breath and I walked through the door. The sun was beaming through the kitchen window as my mother stood at the stove preparing dinner, and my father sat at the dining table, watching the afternoon news on the second smaller TV that was up against the brown brick wall. The smell of my mother's delicious bolognese sauce filled the kitchen; she has always been such a great cook.

It was a normal afternoon scene and if it had been a normal day, I would have grabbed a drink and snack from the fridge and run out into the backyard to play with the dog, before my brother and I would have jumped on our bikes and ridden around the streets of Geelong, always making sure we were home just before dinner.

As if I wanted to rip off the bandaid super quick to lessen the pain, I blurted my news out as fast as I could and without even taking a breath.

I said to my parents that I wasn't going back to school to finish my final year of school and complete Year 12; instead, I had decided I was leaving school and taking a full-time job in retail as a sales assistant.

The disappointment was transparent on both of their faces.

Dad was the first to speak. 'Why would you want to work as a sales assistant? You need to finish your education if you want to get a good job. You're a smart girl – you could be anything you want to be! A doctor, a lawyer, a vet...'

These were all the things my dad wanted me to be.

My mum echoed his thoughts, in a much gentler tone of voice.
She also pointed out that I only had one year left of school before
I graduated, and then I could go to university and become anything
I wanted to be. I could get a real job and have a career – something she
had never had the opportunity to do.

That night – which should have been a normal evening dinner with
lots of chatter, banter, laughter and my brother playing practical jokes on
everyone as usual – was very sombre. There was little conversation and
the mood was serious.

After dinner ended, I went straight to my room. The excitement and
adrenaline that had been running through my veins hours before had been
extinguished. I cried myself to sleep that night, knowing that my parents
were in the lounge room not more than 20 feet away, sharing with each
other how disappointed they were in me. Talking about how hard they
had worked to send us to good schools, to give me a great education –
something that both of them were denied – and this is how I repaid them?
By giving all of it up to go and sell jeans on a shop floor as a sales assistant?

When I woke up the next morning, I knew breakfast was well
underway; Saturdays were always a morning feast in our home. The
smell of crispy bacon and eggs drifted through the whole house.

As I slid open the brown wooden door, I felt all eyes on me. This was
my real-life sliding doors moment. I could still see the sadness in their
eyes, but even in that moment of disappointment, my parents found a
way to encourage me.

'Be passionate, love what you do, work hard and never give up,'
my dad said.

My mum followed it up with, 'Your superpower has always been
to fly. No matter what you do, you will always fly high.' (More on
superpowers in the next chapter.)

And that's how my career began. It definitely was not the decision
my parents wanted me to make. But there I was, just about to turn 17,
with no formal schooling qualification, about to enter the world of retail.

'Be passionate,
love what you do, work hard
and never give up,'
my dad said.

I started out as a sales assistant but I was very quickly promoted to store manager, because I was passionate and I worked hard – just as my parents had modelled for me. It paid off.

You might think I had aspirations of being the CEO one day, and that I was driven by the idea of future promotions. Perhaps, in the back of my mind, that may have been true. But it was really much simpler than that for me.

I loved serving customers and achieving my sales targets. I had a flair for merchandising and I loved dressing the mannequins in the window. I went over and above to please my manager, even if that meant coming in early and staying back late until everything was done.

I would never take a break before my manager had taken hers. Just like I did when working for my parents at the pool canteen, I wanted to make my manager proud.

I noticed that it was often the people who shouted the loudest who were the ones to get noticed, but that just wasn't me. I was a shy teenager, so I knew I needed to get noticed through my results. So that's what I did. I got noticed by breaking sales records, winning competitions, nurturing talent and creating winning teams.

At the age of 20, I became one of the youngest area managers in the group, overseeing 16 stores. At 24, I was appointed to the role of Victorian sales manager, overseeing 54 stores and with three area managers reporting to me.

I had always dreamed of working at Sportsgirl, a brand I loved and had grown up with, so in June 1999 when I was approached to join the brand, it was an opportunity I couldn't refuse. This is where I have spent the last 20 years of my retail career, the last 13 of those years as CEO across Sportsgirl and Sussan.

You don't need a title to be a leader, and, as my sliding doors moment shows, you don't need to know where your path will take you when you start out. When you find something you're truly passionate about, the opportunities for growth will find you.

As I look back on my 30-year retail career, I still see that little girl on the worksite with her father, kitted out in brown cord pants, a hand-knitted brown jumper, black gumboots and with curly blonde hair. Always aiming to please. Always working her very hardest.

I am still that same girl, only now I am a woman – wiser, more experienced and more determined than ever to act as a role model and mentor for other women.

Three

FINDING YOUR SUPERPOWER

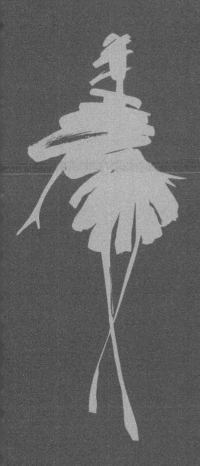

*Love what you do;
do what you love.*

WAYNE DYER

Every woman has a superpower. You might not have discovered yours yet, but I can promise you, you do have one!

So, what's your superpower? What is your unique leadership ID – that 'thing' that has been with you throughout your whole life and that shows up again and again to help give you that edge?

As a child, I had a recurring dream that I could fly. We lived in a two-storey brick house and I would always fly out my bedroom door, down the stairwell and into the lounge room.

I would always share my dream with Mum over the breakfast bench, convinced that it was true. One day, my mum said, 'This must be your superpower!' Mum always humoured and nurtured my every dream – perhaps that was *her* superpower?

What I realised later in life was that I indeed do have the power to fly. I can create my own wings and fly as high as I want to go in life. Obviously, I don't mean literally – but, figuratively, I have a real gift for seeing and leveraging opportunities, for giving things my best and feeling in my bones that the sky is the limit in terms of the life I can create.

I also realised that this superpower extended to others, because I often saw the potential in others, and loved nothing more than the chance to inspire those around me, and watch them shine and achieve their goals, too.

When we think about superpowers, we tend to think of the famous superheroes who save the world in movies and comic books with their strength and powers: Wonder Woman, Captain Marvel or Storm, the Invisible Woman. We have all joked around and asked each other, 'What would your superpower be if you had one?'

Well, the great news is... you already have your own superpower! And I'm going to help you unlock it.

In every superheroine story, there is a problem to solve and a superheroine with just the right skills to do the job.

Wonder woman
is not a fictional
character.
Wonder woman
is a mindset.

UNKNOWN

Heroines all have one thing in common: passion. That's what makes them 'super'. This passion drives them to make a positive impact on the world around them. Every heroine also has unique strengths that they turn to in order to fight the battle and save the day.

In solving a problem, making a positive impact or fighting your battle, you need to know what *your* unique strengths are. They are the positive parts of your personality that increase your ability to face multiple problems and challenges every day.

Now, while the superheroines we've all grown up with are able to become invisible, teleport, breathe underwater or fly, these are just their *exterior* superpowers. When you look more closely, their powers actually go much deeper than what we might first see.

Let's look at Wonder Woman. A tower of strength, she uses her iconic bulletproof bracelets to deflect bullets, her golden lasso of truth for good, and her ability to fly to rescue others.

These are the superpowers we see – but her *real* superpowers are lurking a little under the surface. It's all well and good to be able to teleport, for instance, but if you use that superpower to avoid challenges and get out of sticky situations, then you're not doing much to help yourself or save the world, are you?

That's why I see Wonder Woman as having a raft of different superpowers, which are actually so much more powerful than those on the surface. She is strong, brave, fast and smart. She is a champion of love, peace and truth, and she has a courageous sense of justice. All of these superpowers are used to make a positive impact on the world.

Meanwhile, Supergirl has X-ray vision and can fly and race around at a super speed. But she, too, fights for truth and social justice while protecting the earth. Her real gift is that she uses her powers to make a difference.

1. WHAT AM I PASSIONATE ABOUT?

I value accomplishment and growth and I enjoy having a big career. But what I realised over time was that my true passion was people, and as I moved up the corporate ladder I realised that this was my motivation for growth.

My growth was about growing others. Each promotion was an opportunity to influence, nurture, empower and inspire more people. I especially loved to work with other women and help them grow in their own careers. This has led to me becoming passionate about helping other women believe in themselves, find their superpowers and lead with confidence in their own lives – both at work and personally.

When I talk about passions, I mean the things that really get your heart racing or put a fire in your belly; the things you look forward to the most and that make you feel excited. Do you love giving back and volunteering with charities? Do you love creating amazing pieces of art that bring joy into people's homes? Are you committed to building your career and passionate about your industry? Have you got children whose little minds you love being able to shape?

> To succeed, you have to believe
> in something with such a passion
> that it becomes a reality.
>
> ANITA RODDICK

Think about the things you do, the interactions you have and the moments in your day or your week where you truly feel alive, aligned and on purpose. This is likely to be your passion.

My example: I am passionate about women believing in themselves and leading with confidence in their own lives.

2. WHAT ARE MY TOP THREE STRENGTHS?

We all have our own unique strengths. Think about what comes easily to you: your natural strengths and the things you do well. Call them gifts, talents, skills, knowledge or even quirks – we all have them. Knowing your strengths is key to unlocking your true potential.

Your strengths are part of what makes up your superpower. Once you know your strengths, you can use them to live your best life and bring value to the world.

> It is in herself she will find her strength,
> the strength she needs.

TYLER KNOTT GREGSON

To help you figure out your top three strengths, I've included a list at the end of this chapter. Highlight or circle any that resonate with you, and then whittle that list down to the top three.

My example: My strengths are inspiring others, kindness and authenticity.

3. WHAT AM I MOST KNOWLEDGEABLE ABOUT? WHAT DO I LOVE DOING?

This doesn't have to be related to your job. You might work in a corporate accounting job, but that doesn't mean you have to list 'accounting' or 'tax' as what you're most knowledgeable about. It could be problem-solving, being empathetic to others, your love of learning, nurturing others, your ability to think strategically, or a range of other things.

My example: I am knowledgeable about leadership and business and love to empower and inspire others.

4. NOW COMBINE YOUR ANSWERS INTO A SHORT SENTENCE

Take a blank piece of paper and begin writing down your answers just as I have done. Using words from your answers, start writing a short sentence to unlock your superpower. Keep rewriting your sentence until it feels right – as if it captures the essence of what you are most passionate about.

My example: My superpower is to empower and inspire women to believe in themselves and lead with confidence in business and in life.

Whittled down to one word, my superpower is to *inspire*. I bring out the best in others and encourage them to discover and use their own superpower.

It's time to find your superpower and share it with the world! Check the list on pages 40–41 and circle the words that describe your power.

What is your superpower?

Here's how to figure it out in four easy steps:

1. Write down your passion.

   _____

   _____

   _____

   _____

2. List your top three strengths.

   _____

   _____

   _____

3. Add what you are *most* knowledgeable about or *love* doing.

   _____

   _____

   _____

   _____

4. Combine your answers from questions 1, 2 and 3 into a short sentence to find your superpower!

   _____

   _____

   _____

   _____

Which of these describes you?

Adaptable	Consistent	Firm
Admirable	Cooperative	Flexible
Adventurous	Courageous	Focused
Ambitious	Creative	Forgiving
Authentic	Curious	Friendly
Balanced	Daring	Fun-loving
Brilliant	Decisive	Generous
Calm	Disciplined	Gentle
Capable	Dynamic	Genuine
Caring	Efficient	Gracious
Challenging	Empathetic	Hardworking
Charming	Empowering	Harmonious
Collaborative	Energetic	Helpful
Committed	Enthusiastic	Honest
Communicator	Extraordinary	Humble
Compassionate	Fair	Humorous
Confident	Faithful	Idealistic

Imaginative	Modest	Responsible
Inclusive	Objective	Self-reliant
Independent	Observant	Selfless
Innovative	Open	Sensitive
Insightful	Optimistic	Serious
Inspiring	Organised	Sharing
Integrity	Passionate	Sociable
Intelligent	Patient	Spontaneous
Intuitive	Perfectionist	Strong
Kind	Personable	Studious
Knowledgeable	Playful	Sympathetic
Listener	Practical	Tolerant
Logical	Realistic	Transparent
Loving	Relationships	Trusting
Loyal	Reliable	Understanding
Mature	Resilience	Visionary
Methodical	Respectful	Vulnerable

Hopefully, you have considered the attributes on the previous pages. Did you circle the words that you relate to?

Check the words that you circled; these describe your power. Write this superpower(s) below.

My superpower is...

_____

_____

_____

_____

_____

Then, next time someone asks you what you do, don't reel off the multiple hats that you wear (marketing assistant, sports coach, teacher, mother, wife, boss). Instead, share your superpower.

Just like the superheroines discussed earlier, you too can have a positive impact and change the world with your superpower.

Four

THE POWER OF
CONFIDENCE

Confidence is not
'They will like me'.
Confidence is
'I'll be fine even
if they don't'.

CHRISTINA GRIMMIE

Have you ever met somebody, either in a social or professional situation, and been in awe of how much confidence they have? Did you then walk away and tell yourself, 'She was probably born confident', 'She's obviously an extrovert' or 'She must be an overachiever'?

People might look at me and think, *She is so confident, she must really have her life sorted. She has been a successful CEO, has a beautiful family, has started a number of successful businesses, has a nice house near the beach, she's fit and healthy... I bet she was born with confidence!*

The truth is, none of us are born with confidence.

> ## No-one is born with self confidence. Self confidence is learned and earned with experience.
>
> DENIS WAITLEY

We all suffer from confidence issues, a lack of self-belief and 'imposter syndrome' at different points in our lives. I know I have. Some of us suffer a lot and some suffer a little, but lack of confidence shows up in even the most seemingly confident people.

I have suffered from confidence issues and self-doubt – we all do. Whether that's been walking into a boardroom of strangers and asking myself, 'Should I be here? Am I good enough?', doing a presentation and wondering if my audience was engaged, or meeting new people and wondering if they liked me.

I've experienced many of these moments over the years, and I didn't realise that lack of confidence and self-doubt were so widespread and common until I launched my Mentor Me program. Every single beautiful woman who has participated in my program or I have mentored has revealed that they lack confidence and experience self-doubt, either in their personal lives, career, appearance or the way they see themselves compared to others.

Women seem particularly prone to experiencing confidence issues that hold them back. Research shows that men apply for a job or promotion when they meet only 60 per cent of the required qualifications, whereas women apply only if they meet 100 per cent of them. This is because men overestimate their abilities and performance, and women often do the opposite.

Meanwhile, 67 per cent of women reported they needed support building confidence to feel like they could become leaders, according to KPMG's women leadership study.

Women also tend to ask for fewer pay rises than men – the same KPMG study found that women ask for a pay boost four times less often than men. Men not only negotiate pay rises more frequently but also negotiate harder, requesting 30 per cent more than women do. But that's a story for a whole other book!

As a CEO I have spent my entire career inspiring and empowering women to believe in themselves, so I didn't realise what a common theme this is among women. I have either done a great job building a team of confident women, or I had my confidence blinkers on!

Of course, as I mentioned, I've had my own experiences with sneaky imposter syndrome and self-doubt. I remember the first charity event that my husband and I did together. It was a 50 km Coastrek – a team trekking challenge.

We had trained in the lead up, eaten well and done all the right things to prepare for this massive physical challenge. A week out from the event, I broke down and told my husband he needed to find a new partner to do it with.

'I can't do it,' I confided. 'I'm not going to be able to complete it and I'm going to let you down.'

I felt like I wasn't good enough. I had convinced myself that I was going to fail and disappoint my husband, because self-doubt and a lack of confidence had taken over my mind.

Luckily, I have a supportive husband who has endless belief in me and who convinced me otherwise.

'What are you scared of?' he asked me.

The truth was that I wasn't scared of letting him down; I was scared of failing.

Needless to say, we did the Coastrek... in fact, we smashed it! That experience gave me the confidence to complete more events over the years.

It all started with me overcoming my self-doubt and believing in myself – something that I was able to do because I put in the work and had the willingness to try.

MY CONFIDENCE TRANSFORMATION

My evolution from a shy teenager to a confident CEO has been a long and winding path. From standing out the front of a Sportsgirl store not even having the confidence to walk in as a shopper, to becoming the CEO of the brand and leading it towards growth and success – well, let's just say that transformation didn't happen overnight!

I vividly remember gazing longingly through the windows of the Sportsgirl store in my hometown of Geelong when I was around 13 or 14. I couldn't bring myself to step inside.

I told myself the story that I didn't fit in: I wasn't pretty enough or tall enough; I didn't have perfect blonde hair, I wasn't a size eight and I was introverted. All of the sales assistants looked so glamorous and were outgoing and confident.

I was the total opposite: a shy, quiet teenager who was happiest hanging onto my mother's apron strings. I had huge self-doubt and low confidence and felt I was never smart enough, fast enough, tall enough or skinny enough. My mum was my safety net: she was the electric fence that no-one could get past and she would always protect me.

Having a lack of confidence can have a dramatic effect on our careers and relationships. It prevents us from putting our hands up for promotions, trying new things, speaking our truth and truly valuing ourselves.

It often keeps us in our safe lane – the one where we feel most comfortable (because we are scared of failure).

A lack of confidence might be the reason a good friend stays in a toxic relationship or your sister constantly underplays her skills and abilities even though she is a successful businesswoman. Or the reason a colleague doesn't put her hand up for a promotion, even though she has all the skills. One of the reasons we don't go after what we really want in life is that we don't actually believe we deserve it.

We are all terrified of failure or rejection. It's natural. But when we gain confidence, we're able to circle around those fears – we never get rid of them altogether, but we try regardless.

How does that saying go, again? Feel the fear and do it anyway.

My journey towards confidence has been a long one, with many experiences along the way that moved me towards the point where I could approach a boardroom and kill the self-doubt before I stepped through the door. I was really fortunate to have an incredible role model in the early days of my career – not that I really knew what role models were back then. All I knew was that Vivienne, my area manager, supported me, guided me, encouraged me and often pushed me outside of my comfort zone. She was 10 years older than me and full of wisdom. She was funny, loud, caring and confident, and I loved everything about her. I wanted to be like her.

I remember she called to tell me she was going to be visiting the store the following day and would like to take me out for a coffee. I didn't sleep a wink that night; I kept thinking, *Why is she coming to take me out for a coffee? What have I done wrong? Am I in trouble for something?!*

Being Little Miss Goody Two Shoes, the idea of upsetting or disappointing someone was my worst-case scenario – I was a pleaser, remember! So this was the story I was telling myself. Self-doubt and a lack of confidence was running rampant inside my head.

However, the story I was telling myself couldn't have been further from the truth. She wanted to take me for coffee to offer me my first managerial role... and I was just 18 years old! I felt an explosion of excitement and nerves course through me – and then came the crushing, familiar weight of self-doubt. Am I capable? Can I do it? What if I'm not good enough? What if I fail?

What Vivienne said next will always stay with me.

I believe in you; now you need to believe in yourself.

These words were like magic and I've never forgotten them. They're words that I have said to myself over and over again, and words that I have said to others as well.

It is amazing what we are capable of when we have self-belief. Vivienne was one of many mentors I've had over the years who have helped me to believe in myself, and I'm thrilled to now be a mentor who helps other women to see just how valuable they are – and how much they have to offer the world.

WHAT IS CONFIDENCE?

Before we get into what confidence is, I want to start with what confidence is *not*.

Confidence is not...

- ◇ Faking it till you make it
- ◇ Trying to be someone else or someone you're not
- ◇ Being arrogant or rude
- ◇ Shifting responsibility
- ◇ Fearing being wrong
- ◇ Judging others
- ◇ Thinking you are the smartest person in the room
- ◇ Having an over-inflated ego or opinion of yourself

We need to be confident in our abilities as women so that we can achieve the goals and dreams we set for ourselves. Once we believe we can, we are more likely to make those goals and dreams a reality.

When we don't feel confident, it is easy to self-sabotage and compare ourselves to other women's lives and success. We tell ourselves that these women:

- speak up in meetings
- express their opinions
- put themselves forward for a promotion
- rarely think they are not good enough
- are confident in their own skin
- live the perfect life.

The truth is, I've never met anyone who ticks all of these boxes. Even the most confident women have self-doubt.

A lack of confidence is one of the core issues that holds us back, both personally and professionally. But what is it that causes our confidence to be eroded, and what can we do about it?

Self-confidence
is a superpower.
Once you start to
believe in yourself,
magic starts
happening.

ANONYMOUS

Fear of being judged

A lack of confidence often comes from a fear of being judged – and it is common among women. It is linked to our natural desire to be liked and prevents us from speaking up, asking for help and sharing our opinions and ideas. This fear, in most cases, is a reflection of our own insecurities. We judge ourselves on what we think is acceptable. Often when people are judging others, it's to make themselves feel better because they are lacking self-acceptance and self-love. I believe if we could all learn to love ourselves we would live with more compassion and less judgement.

> ## Do you fear being judged, or are you judging yourself unconsciously?
>
> VARSHA SAKHRANI

What you can do:

- Know your values and stand by them.
- Be your authentic self and be comfortable in your own skin.
- Never take judgement personally. You know yourself better than anyone else. Don't let others define you.
- Take feedback and criticism onboard. See it as a way to grow.

What fears keep you stuck? Are you worried about what others say or think of you? Do you judge others harshly? If not, why do you expect others to judge you?

_____

_____

_____

Lack of self-belief

If you don't believe in yourself, no-one else will. The way you see yourself, believe in yourself, talk to yourself and think of yourself will also affect the way others see you. Without the ability to believe in your own worth, you can often set the benchmark low and rob yourself of reaching your full potential.

Self-belief starts from within.

> ## Nothing holds us back more than our own insecurities.
>
> KUSH AND WIZDOM

What you can do:

- Back yourself. Be your own biggest fan and talk to yourself as you would to your best friend.
- Surround yourself with your cheer squad.
- Don't compare yourself to others; there is only ever going to be one of you.
- Celebrate your efforts as well as your accomplishments.

Ask yourself ...

What areas in life are you really good at? This could be anything from being an inspiring leader, a loving parent, to an accomplished athlete. Where do you have strong self-belief and where do you struggle?

_____

_____

_____

What you tell yourself
every day will either
lift you up or
tear you down.

SHARIFAH NOR

Listening to your inner critic

We all have one! Women tend to manage their inner self-critic less effectively than men do, in which case the inner critic becomes stronger. The more you entertain your inner critic, the stronger it becomes. It's like feeding the beast. The inner critic voice often says things like, 'What's wrong with me?' 'As if I am capable of that!' 'Why did I say that?' 'I don't deserve this success.'

The inner critic can hold us back from achieving our goals and dreams.

What you can do:

- Question your inner critic: is this really true? Or just a story I'm telling myself?
- Catch your inner critic when it becomes active and change the story.
- Stop overthinking; wallowing in your thoughts allows your inner critic to become active.
- Build in a daily practice of gratitude. This will promote positive self-talk and thinking.

Ask yourself ...

What does your inner critic say about you? Why do you believe it? If you chose NOT to believe your inner critic, what story could you tell yourself instead?

_____

_____

_____

_____

_____

Fear of embarrassment

We often feel embarrassed when we believe we have not lived up to expectations – especially those we put on ourselves. We are afraid that people will think badly of us and judge us, and that we won't measure up compared to others. The thought of being embarrassed or humiliated prevents us from saying yes, making the most of opportunities and taking healthy risks. No-one else expects you to be Wonder Woman!

> ## If you're never scared or embarrassed or hurt it means you never take any chances.
>
> JULIA SORE

What you can do:

- Learn how to become comfortable in the uncomfortable.
- Allow yourself to become more vulnerable. What makes you vulnerable also makes you beautiful.
- Don't be afraid to share your feelings and talk through what happened.
- Own your mistakes. This shows self-awareness, authenticity and courage.

Ask yourself ...

What are you most afraid of? What's the worst that can happen? Do you judge others when they do something 'embarrassing'? How can you recover from an embarrassing moment?

_____

_____

_____

Fear of appearing arrogant

Fear of appearing arrogant prevents a lot of women from being more engaged, speaking up in meetings, asking direct questions and putting themselves out there. However, there is a huge difference between confidence and arrogance. Arrogant people act as if they are superior and more valuable or important than others, and believe they know more than everyone else. Confident people believe in themselves and their abilities, feel comfortable in their own skin and know their true worth. Confident people are great listeners and are always willing to learn from others.

> Don't be arrogant, because arrogance
> kills curiosity and passion.
>
> MINA BISSELL

What you can do:
- Celebrate and shine the light on others' success.
- Talk less about yourself and ask more questions of others.
- Don't be afraid to be wrong or not have all the answers.
- Know your strengths and limitations.

Why do you have this belief that confidence equals arrogance? What is the worst thing that could happen if someone perceived you as arrogant? Can you think of examples of women who you believe are confident without being arrogant?

_____

_____

_____

Don't wait for
the stars to align,
reach up and
rearrange them
the way you want...
create your own
constellation.

Waiting for the stars to align

We can all think of a time in our lives when we've thought the timing just isn't right. 'I'll wait until the kids are a bit older.' 'I'll wait until we are more financially stable.' 'I'll wait until I'm 100 per cent prepared.' (This is a common one among women.) The truth is, there's never going to be that 'perfect time'. There's always going to be something else that comes up or another excuse that will get in the way – and you'll still be waiting for that ideal time to start, which may never come.

What you can do:

- Realise you don't need to be perfect – you just need to start.
- Stop making excuses. While you are waiting for the stars to align, someone else is living out your hopes and dreams.
- Ask yourself what you are really afraid of. What's the worst thing that could happen?
- Visualise yourself as you want to be. We can't be what we can't see!
- Force yourself to get outside your comfort zone and you'll realise what you are really capable of.

Ask yourself ...

Think of something in your life that you have on hold. What are the barriers standing in the way right now (real or perceived)? How can you start working to remove some of these? What steps would you take to reach your goals if these barriers didn't exist?

_____

_____

_____

_____

_____

Guilt

As women, we often feel guilty about taking care of ourselves, so we tend to put ourselves last. We're reluctant to do anything that might seem self-indulgent. This is often because we tell ourselves that we have other priorities and more important things to do. We can also feel guilty about having said the wrong thing to a friend, for not calling our mother this week, because there's nothing in the fridge for dinner, because we've forgotten to send a birthday card or because we mixed up the kids' lunch boxes.

Guilt is the thief of life.

ANTHONY HOPKINS

What you can do:

- Prioritise your own self-care. You can only be good to others when you are good to yourself first.
- Stop telling yourself stories that are not true; we should never feel guilty about making decisions to take care of ourselves.
- Appreciate yourself and all that you do. Write a self-gratitude diary at the end of each day or make a note in your phone to get into the practice of focusing on what you *did* achieve.

Ask yourself ...

Consider something in your life that you feel guilty about. Where does this feeling come from? Is it real – do you genuinely have something to feel guilty about, or is it a story you are telling yourself? What can you do to remove the unnecessary guilt from the situation?

_____

_____

SIX CONFIDENCE MYTHS

There are so many myths about confidence. If we start to believe these myths, we can find ourselves living with self-doubt and self-sabotage. We can even begin to feel that confidence is out of reach for us.

Strive for progress not for perfection.

BECKY BURSELL

I want to share with you six of the biggest confidence myths I've encountered throughout my life. It's time to squash these misconceptions and allow yourself to feel confident inside so you can move forward and live your best life.

MYTH 1: You are born with confidence

Nobody is born with confidence; it's something we develop and strive for as we go through life and experience new situations and environments.

The good news is that confidence is a skill that can be learnt. Like any new skill, it takes time and effort to grow and nourish it. The more you practise, the easier it becomes. Like a muscle, the more we use it the stronger our confidence becomes.

When we confront challenging situations, push ourselves out of our comfort zones and do things we never imagined or thought possible, we are building confidence.

MYTH 2: You either have it or you don't

There will be times in your life when you feel full of confidence – like you could take on the world and achieve anything you put your mind to. Then there'll be other times when uncertainty and self-doubt take over.

If you are a confident person this week or this month, that doesn't necessarily mean this will be the case next week or next month.

Confidence shows up at different times throughout our lives. It can be situational. When good things happen – such as winning a new client, meeting our seasonal sales target or getting asked out on a first date – our confidence builds. When not-so-good things happen – such as losing the race, getting dumped by a partner, missing out on a promotion or receiving a customer complaint – our confidence plummets. When we acknowledge that confidence is situational, we are better equipped to deal with good and bad situations.

MYTH 3: Extroverts are more confident

When we think about a confident person, we often picture someone who is highly extroverted. However, extroverts don't necessarily have more confidence than introverts; they are often just louder!

Being extroverted or introverted has nothing to do with confidence – it's all about what energises or drains us. An introvert who has strong values, knows what she stands for and is self-aware can be just as confident as an extrovert.

So, it doesn't matter whether your personality leans more towards introversion or extroversion – we all have the ability to build confidence. It's like anything in life: it starts with us and it takes practice.

MYTH 4: It has to be perfect before I start

Whether it be applying for a promotion, starting your own business or training for a marathon, women often feel everything needs to be perfect before taking that scary step. This diminishes our confidence and prevents us from achieving what we set out to do.

We need to change the story we are telling ourselves. If it's something that is important to us and really matters, confidence builds with the willingness to try. When we do what matters, the confidence will flow.

When we strive for perfection, however, we end up disappointing ourselves. This is one of the biggest confidence killers. We need to move from striving for perfect to having a go and doing our best.

MYTH 5: Only achievement builds confidence

We all want to achieve great things in life: building a billion-dollar empire, climbing Mount Everest, winning a grand slam, breaking a world record or writing a bestselling book.

While all of these achievements are extraordinary, they are big events and won't happen for many of us. But does that mean we shouldn't feel confidence in ourselves?

We can build confidence daily by acknowledging our small achievements. When we notice the small wins in our everyday lives, we are building our confidence and self-worth.

Supporting a friend in need, cooking a great meal, taking time out for yourself, running that extra kilometre you didn't think you could run, improving on your previous exam score or getting that marketing pitch across the line are all achievements to celebrate. Focus on the little wins as well as the big ones. They all help to build your confidence and self-worth, and validate all the great things you have to offer to the world. Small achievements can give us the confidence to build up to extraordinary achievements.

MYTH 6: When I'm confident, I won't feel insecure or afraid

Confidence does not mean the absence of fear or insecurities. Life throws us many curve balls and challenges, and feeling insecure or afraid is part of being human.

Feeling anxious or nervous is a normal reaction to taking a risk or trying something new. It could be changing jobs, moving to a new school, jumping out of a plane or meeting your new partner's family for the first time. When we step out of our comfort zone and walk into the unknown, we build new skills as we go. Like anything we do for the first time, it can feel uncomfortable and we can feel afraid.

Building confidence starts with a willingness to **try**. When we **try**, we **build skills**. When we **build skills**, we **build competency**. When we **build competency**, we **build confidence**.

Real confidence starts with you

A confident woman uses positive words to build herself and others up.

A confident woman doesn't need to put others down to feel good about herself.

A confident woman leaves you feeling inspired after your conversation.

A confident woman knows what her strengths are.

A confident woman focuses on what's in her control.

A confident woman creates her own success without tearing others down.

A confident woman takes responsibility rather than ascribing blame.

A confident woman has put in the work.

A confident woman understands the importance of self-care.

A confident woman knows when to say 'no'.

A confident woman listens more than she talks.

A confident woman has clear goals and takes action to achieve them.

A confident woman is happy to learn from others.

Ask yourself ...

What does confidence mean to you?

_____

_____

_____

_____

_____

_____

_____

_____

I want you to think for a minute about your own self-confidence. How confident do you feel around your work? What about your confidence when you are with friends and your family? How confident do you feel about making a presentation at work or talking to a stranger?

_____

_____

_____

_____

_____

_____

_____

_____

HOW TO BUILD CONFIDENCE

To be confident means living a life of fulfilment, passion and purpose. Building confidence is a work in progress – and no matter how big or small the steps, progress is progress.

> ## The most beautiful thing you can wear is confidence.
>
> BLAKE LIVELY

There are many things we can do to build our confidence. Some of them are just small changes to our mindset and others we have to work on for a bit longer to create new habits. No matter what, building confidence starts with the decision to take *action!*

When we hear the words 'confident woman', most of us will immediately picture a particular person we know. This woman stands out; she oozes positivity and success and radiates happiness. She is our ideal and perfect picture of confidence.

But what is it about these people that makes them confident? I believe if someone seems to have incredible self-confidence, it's because they have worked on building it all of their life.

As with most traits, there are certain things you can apply to your life and build on to becoming a more confident woman every day and increase your happiness and live the life you want to live.

Confidence is not something that we can build overnight; it is a process and takes practice. Let's take a look at a few ways to increase your self-confidence and help you go after the things you want out of life.

**Confidence starts internally.
It starts with self!**

Confidence is...

- ✧ The ability to turn your thoughts into actions
- ✧ The decision to try
- ✧ A feeling of self-assurance that comes from an appreciation of your abilities or qualities
- ✧ Showing up as your most authentic self
- ✧ Stepping outside your comfort zone
- ✧ Owning your mistakes
- ✧ Embracing your purpose
- ✧ Shining the spotlight on others
- ✧ Seeking approval from only the people who really matter
- ✧ Doing what is right, not what is popular
- ✧ Being willing to take risks
- ✧ Being able to accept a compliment
- ✧ Taking action, despite your fears
- ✧ Standing up for your beliefs
- ✧ Freely asking for help

Confidence is contagious

Confidence is contagious, just like negativity is contagious.

When you surround yourself with other like-minded and confident women, it is like having a massive surge of positivity thrown into your day.

Sure, we all have bad days, and life is not always going to be rainbows and unicorns. But when you are able to find the positive in (almost) every situation, it leaves you feeling empowered and inspired. Spending time around confident people who live by the same philosophy is likely to rub off on you and help you build your own confidence.

It's also important to limit your time with the negative people you let in to your life. There is no place for toxic people in the life of a confident woman.

Your words become your actions

A single word or sentence has the power to change your mood. It can set off a negative mindset or boost your confidence. It's important to practise using words that help us build our confidence.

Start telling yourself, 'I am a kind and helpful woman, I am great at my job, I am worthy, I am a loyal friend, I can achieve this, I'm going to apply for that promotion, I deserve it'. Positive language will have a positive impact on your day and on those around you.

A confident woman also uses positive words in her conversations to build herself and others up. She doesn't have to put other people down in order for her to feel good about herself.

A conversation with a confident woman will leave you feeling inspired.

Self-care is not selfish

Confidence requires us to take care of ourselves before we take care of those around us. In my early years of travelling, I was always perplexed as to why airline staff would advise adult plane passengers to put their own oxygen mask on first before helping others. As a mother I thought this was selfish. Of course I'm going to put masks on my children before myself! However, I soon realised that we need to take care of ourselves so that we can best take care of others – not just when flying but also in life.

Grinding ourselves to the bone just leads to resentment, exhaustion and sometimes burnout – I know because I've been there. Schedule in regular self-care activities – even if it means getting up half an hour earlier, just so you can sit and enjoy that first cup of coffee, write in your journal or go for a walk with the dog.

Self-care is also about asking for help when you need it. We don't often do this because we think we need to be independent – otherwise we'll be seen as weak or failing.

Change your story

We are constantly creating stories as our minds try to make sense of what's happening around us. We have 6000 thoughts going through our minds every day.

We are continually tapping into our past, which shapes our beliefs about who we are, what we believe to be true, what we are capable of and what we think we deserve. The stories we tell ourselves can negatively affect our confidence.

That inner critical voice inside our heads that I talked about earlier is highly judgemental and can leave us feeling miserable and stuck. It can even sabotage our success.

What stories does your inner critical voice tell you? See if any of the following sound familiar:

- I'm going to fail.
- I feel guilty.
- I'm underprepared.
- I don't fit in.
- I need more skills.
- I'm not good enough.

We need to interrupt these stories from taking control and create a more empowering story that helps us feel confident to take action. **Change your story – change your life!**

Embrace your strengths and weaknesses

An important part of building confidence and knowing and appreciating who we are is recognising our strengths and weaknesses. When we are aware of these, we can work with them and use them to our advantage.

Most of us tend to focus on our shortcomings or weaknesses and forget about our strengths. This only contributes to our lack of confidence. It's important to have a balanced view of our strengths and weaknesses.

We all have weaknesses. Some of mine include being a perfectionist, overcommitting and saying 'yes' when I really want to say 'no'. Knowing your weaknesses gives you a clearer understanding of things that may be holding you back, and areas you would like to work on.

Identifying our strengths is also important. Knowing what we're good at helps us to live with passion and purpose, and increases our confidence. Embracing our strengths brings joy to our lives and to those around us. My strengths include being resilient, multitasking, inspiring and empowering others, and being a caring and authentic human.

In your daily life, choose one strength to embrace and one weakness to improve on.

Go for it!

In life there are always people who'll tell you that you can't accomplish your goals and dreams – whether that's your employer, a teacher, a friend or a family member. People will try to tell you your goal is too big or crazy, that you're not ready or that you can't do it.

Don't listen to them! Go for it! Women are changing the world every day, despite everyone around them telling them it can't be done.

That promotion you have been waiting to apply for... Go for it! That online business you have been wanting to start... Go for it! Those five kilos you have been wanting to lose... Go for it! That person you have been wanting to ask on a date... Go for it!

If you think you can do it, you can.

Be kind to yourself

Start eliminating negative thoughts you have about yourself. If someone gives you a compliment, accept it! Make a list of your skills and remind yourself of your own value and worth.

Instead of beating yourself up about not being an amazing cook, tell yourself what a great mum you are. Instead of being harsh on yourself because you aren't great at spreadsheets, remind yourself how much your team trusts you. Every day, think about the things that make you unique, special and wonderful.

Start your daily routine with the words 'I am'.

My example: I am kind, smart, trustworthy, loyal, funny.

Feeling more confident in yourself needs to start with changing the way you think about yourself, the way you perceive yourself and, most importantly, the way you treat yourself.

Belief starts from within! It starts with you!
Be kind to yourself!

Know your values

When asked about their values, most people don't know them.

Knowing our values is super important if we want to live with confidence. Values support all of our decision-making, both personally and professionally.

But what are values, and why do we need them? Values are the things that are most important in your life – those things that really matter to you. They're the ideas and beliefs that you deem to be most important in the way you live and work.

Your values have likely been influenced by a range of things, including your background, events that have happened or you have witnessed, your upbringing or maybe your spiritual beliefs.

Values give us clarity with our decision-making. Living by our values allows us to feel more content, more confident and more in control, because our decisions are in line with our belief system

Have you ever actioned a decision even though it felt wrong? You didn't know why, but there was something warning you that it wasn't quite right? This is what happens when your decisions don't align with your values. When your decisions don't align with your values, it will feel wrong... because it *is* wrong.

Once you are clear on your values, they will be the gatekeepers for all of your decision-making. I'll share more on values and how to find out what yours are later in the book.

Step out of your comfort zone

Whether you're an extrovert, an introvert or somewhere in between, trying something new or stepping outside of your comfort zone can be tough. You are going to be nervous, anxious and maybe even scared (that's normal). It can help to remember that there are one of two things that can happen: you will succeed or you will fail, and unless you are running off a cliff without a parachute I promise you'll survive.

> ## Everything you have ever wanted
> ## is one step outside of your comfort zone.
>
> ROBERT J ALLEN

If you think about the first time you tried something new – whether that be running your first webinar (I know my first one sucked), riding a bike, making your first dress, writing your first blog post or pitching to your first client – I'm tipping it was pretty awful compared to how it is now you've had practice. This is because the more you do something, the more competent you become.

When we try something new we either **succeed** or **fail** but we survive.
When we **fail** we **learn**.
When we **learn** we are **building skills**.
When we **build skills**, we **gain competency**.
When we **gain competency**, we **gain confidence**.
Confidence begins with the decision and willingness to try!

It is confidence in our bodies,
minds and spirits that
allows us to keep looking
for new adventures.

OPRAH WINFREY

Love yourself

There is one thing that I believe every single human on this planet has in common: the desire to be loved. But love has to start internally. Love has to start with us loving ourselves first.

Compassion, kindness, empathy and affection are not just for us to give to others; we need to offer them to ourselves, too.

Loving ourselves is about self-respect, accepting our imperfections, positive self-talk and strong self-worth. It allows us to stop constantly comparing ourselves to others, celebrate our successes no matter how big or small, accept our failure lessons and move forward.

When we truly love ourselves we build confidence, flourish and shine and live a life of fulfilment and happiness.

Move your thoughts into action

Understand that while your thoughts, ambitions and dreams are important, they don't mean anything unless you move to action!

It's all well and good to say, 'I want to double my business in the next two years' or 'I want to be more present in my relationship' or 'I hate my job and need a new one.' But you need to move these *thoughts* into *action*. You need a plan.

I call it the **what, why, when** and **where to from here**. It's simple and straightforward; it's a matter of taking your goal and setting some tangible tasks and milestones to move it forward.

Take my example of doubling your business in two years:

- **What** is the goal? Doubling your number of clients? Doubling your revenue? Be specific, and then break that one big goal up into smaller monthly or quarterly targets.

- **Why** does it matter? When it matters to you, it becomes a priority. For instance, doubling your clients will boost your income, improve your cash flow, allow you to reinvest and continue to grow and build your reputation in the industry.

- **When** do you want to achieve this goal? Deadlines and timeframes make you more accountable. Don't be vague and say 'within a few months': put a clear date on you goal.
- And, lastly, **where to from here**? These are your actions. What tangible steps can you take to double your clients, for instance? Do you have a marketing and networking strategy? Could you introduce a referral or loyalty program?

Unless you take your thoughts and move them into action, they will be nothing more than dreams.

Celebrate your wins

Are you one of those people who is already looking for the next thing to do the minute you have accomplished a task? It's so easy to forget to stop and take a moment to celebrate your wins.

I'm as guilty of this as anyone else. But when we make the effort to acknowledge our successes – even if they're small – it is incredible the amount of satisfaction, pride and joy we feel.

It's easy to lose confidence when we feel like we haven't achieved anything. I really encourage you to write down one thing each day that is a win (remember, it can be big or small). It could be baking a perfect chocolate cake, finishing a project ahead of schedule, receiving positive feedback at work or getting a pay rise.

Acknowledging your wins fosters a positive mindset and helps build confidence. When you're low in confidence, pull out your list and use it to remind yourself of all the awesome stuff you've done.

I truly believe the universe hands us more when we appreciate and acknowledge what we have.

So, remember to take the time to stop and take a moment to breathe, appreciate, feel gratitude and celebrate your wins.

Five

THE POWER OF LEADERSHIP

Great leaders don't tell you what to do; they show you how it's done.

ALESSANDRO BERSELLI

In the early days of my career, I looked up to and admired people who had fancy titles, levels of authority and positions of power. What I've learnt over time in both business and in life is that somebody's title or rank, level of authority or position of power doesn't automatically qualify them for leadership.

You don't need a title to be a leader. You can be a leader in your family, your classroom, your community, your place of worship, your friendship group, your neighbourhood or your workplace. We all have the ability to be leaders in our own lives.

Supporting someone through challenging times... **is being a leader**.

Inspiring and encouraging others to do their best... **is being a leader**.

Checking in on someone you're worried about... **is being a leader**.

Standing up for what's right... **is being a leader**.

Encouraging teamwork and harmony... **is being a leader**.

Leading a project or task in school... **is being a leader**.

In other words: you don't need to be a CEO to be a leader!

The best leadership I have ever witnessed is where a person has a passion for a cause that is larger than themselves. They are courageous and have a clear vision, integrity, honesty, humility and a strong focus. Great leadership is perhaps the most important competitive advantage an organisation can have.

For me, leadership boils down to the ability to motivate people to go places they would never otherwise go. It is about forming genuine connections with the people I get to inspire every day, empowering and guiding then to accomplish their goals and dreams in business and in life.

I am often asked the question, 'What would you like your leadership legacy to be?' My answer never relates to my legacy in terms of the role or title I have. I want people to remember *me*, the person I am – wife, mother, friend, mentor, daughter, aunty and sister; someone who is strong, inspiring, compassionate and kind. I want people to remember me for the way I made them *feel* and the positive impact I had on their lives.

Every decision, every interaction, every reaction and every action, both at work and in our personal lives, is an expression of the person we are and the world we want to create.

Only when we are being bold, staying true to our values and feeling empowered ourselves can we start to lead others.

WHAT IS LEADERSHIP?

There are as many definitions of leadership as there are leaders. If you google the word 'leadership' you will get millions of results, with each definition as unique as an individual leader. The definition in the English dictionary is:

Leadership

1. The action of leading a group of people or an organisation.
    'Different styles of leadership'

    Similar – guidance, direction, authority, control, management, superintendence, supervision, organization, government, orchestration, initiative, influence

2. The state or position of a leader.
    'The party prospered under his leadership'

    Similar – headship, directorship, governorship, governance, administration, jurisdiction, captaincy, superintendence, control, ascendancy, rule, command, power, mastery, domination, dominion, premiership

I don't know about you, but very few of these words inspire me. I prefer words such as authentic, empowering, inspiring, influential, respectful, kind, confident and passionate.

I want to share with you my very simple definitions of leadership...

◇ **Leadership** is taking care of your people so they can thrive, shine and be at their natural best.

◇ **Leadership** is not necessarily about *you* doing great things – it's encouraging *others* to do great things.

◇ **Leadership** is the ability to guide others into a direction or decision in a way that still leaves them feeling empowered and accomplished.

◇ **Leadership** is leading with your heart, not just your head. It is showing empathy, compassion and courage in the way you lead.

◇ **Leadership** is the ability to translate vision into reality.

◇ **Leadership** is a mindset, a heartset, a behaviour, a feeling and a way of being.

◇ **Leadership** is believing in someone and helping them believe in themselves.

◇ **Leadership** is looking after those to the left of you and those to the right of you.

◇ **Leadership** is a lifestyle choice.

◇ **Leadership** is influence, not authority.

◇ **Leadership** is about unlocking human potential so that others can shine.

◇ **Leadership** is acting in a way that allows others to gain.

◇ **Leadership** is always staying true to your values.

◇ **Leadership** is being someone people choose to follow.

Ask yourself ...

When leading in your own life, whether that's at work or at play, what does leadership truly mean to you?

_____

_____

What are the qualities of a great leader?

_____

_____

What do you want your leadership legacy to be?

_____

_____

Does your leadership style today reflect your values and who you really are?

_____

_____

What do you need to keep doing to be the leader you want to be?

_____

_____

What are three things you can start doing and three things you should stop doing to become the leader you want to be?

Start doing	Stop doing
1. _____	1. _____
2. _____	2. _____
3. _____	3. _____

LEADERSHIP IS A LIFESTYLE CHOICE

Leadership is not easy. It's something you have to practise and work on each and every day.

Just like being a parent, leading a healthy life or being an athlete are lifestyle choices, so too is being a leader.

I have always found many similarities between parenting and leadership. I've applied many of my parental learnings to my role as CEO, as well as my everyday life.

As new parents we dive in, often not knowing what the heck we are doing, working it out as we go. Early leadership can be just like this!

When you first become a parent, you don't get a handbook titled *How to be a Great Parent* and away you go. The same goes with becoming a great leader.

Becoming a parent is one of the most wonderful things that has ever happened to me and I'm sure, if you're a parent, you will agree (most of the time). But being a parent is hard work and there is no one-size-fits-all solution, much like being a leader.

Like most mothers to be, during my pregnancies I read lots of books and magazines, asked questions of mothers I knew (including my own incredible mother) and went to prenatal classes. Although all of the information and advice I received was fabulous at the time, it wasn't until I was in the role of being a parent that I learnt how to become one. I do use the word *learnt*, because that's what I did. I learnt every day. I learnt what to do and what not to do. I made mistakes. I cried, I laughed, I lost my confidence and I built my confidence back up again. My children are now in their teens and early 20s and I'm still learning how to be a parent every day.

You evolve as a parent, just as you evolve as a leader. Each year of parenthood throws you different challenges and as your children grow, so too do you grow as a parent.

The challenges you have as a parent when your children are toddlers are different from when they are teenagers and different again when they become young adults, but for me the approach has always been the same: teach, guide, coach, nurture, encourage, inspire, empower, build their confidence, let them fall and pick them back up. These are the exact same guiding principles I have used throughout my career as a leader and CEO.

Our role as parents and leaders is to create environments where people feel safe and cared for, so they can thrive and shine.

In life, we never stop being students – whether that be students of parenting, philosophy, relationships or leadership. To reap the rewards we have to be willing to learn and put in the work.

There will be days that are tough, days when you wonder what you were thinking and days when you want to give up. But, as with any lifestyle choice, it takes practice, discipline and consistency to see great results. The more practice you put in, the better results you get – and the more that leading with confidence becomes second-nature.

Leadership is a lifestyle choice I have made and one that I choose to be a student of every day.

As leaders, we can't pick and choose which days we feel like giving our best. We do the right thing because we hold ourselves to a high standard.

Leadership is not just behaving in a certain way when the cameras are on. It's not just a 'sometimes' thing. Leadership is a lifestyle!

Living your best leadership life is about:

- building others up
- serving others first
- being courageous
- gaining knowledge and wisdom
- being a team player
- having a positive attitude
- encouraging others
- doing the hard stuff
- listening and learning
- mentoring others.

Being a great leader
requires intention and a
consistent approach to
everything that you do.

When leaders embrace
leadership as a lifestyle, they
show up the same way…

…in the classroom
…at home
…at the office
…in public.

COLLEEN CALLANDER

You cannot *lead* an organisation.

You can *run* an organisation.

You cannot *lead* a project.

You can *manage* a project.

You can only *lead people.*

Leaders lead people.

If you are in a **leadership** role,
then your role is to **lead people.**

LEADING IN YOUR OWN LIFE

I believe that each of us has the ability to be a leader in our own lives – whatever our lifestyle choices. Whether you are a CEO, a mother, a partner, a business owner, an entrepreneur, a coach or a community worker, you can choose the type of leader you want to be.

Throughout my life I have always wanted to inspire, influence and impact those around me to be the best versions of themselves and to live their best lives – whether that be my family, friends or in the working world. Now, in this next chapter of my life as a mentor, a speaker and an author, I want to take the same principles – inspire, influence and impact – so I can support as many women as possible to lead in their own lives. I want women to believe in themselves and know that anything is possible.

Globally, the absence of women in leadership roles is startling and, quite frankly, unacceptable.

I have reflected on what leading means to me, how it shows up in my life and how I can make a positive impact on the world around me. My aim is to encourage and inspire other women to become the leaders they have always wanted to be, to have the confidence to lead in their own lives, and to have a voice.

INSPIRE

To inspire others is to excite, encourage, generate confidence, be selfless and creative, and dare to be different. People who inspire us are people we look up to or admire, or those we would like to emulate. Richard Branson identifies the ability to inspire as the single most important leadership skill.

I ask myself every day,
'Am I being a person who
inspires, influences and
impacts other people's lives
in a positive way?'

COLLEEN CALLANDER

We can inspire those around us by:

- sharing our vision
- living with purpose
- building others up
- creating stretch goals
- working with our people
- investing in our people
- being fearless
- taking action.

Share your vision

As a leader, sharing your vision is essential to inspire those around you and encourage them to focus on what matters most, what you want to accomplish and how you intend to get there. A vision often takes lessons from the past, addresses the present and looks to the future.

When you communicate your vision clearly and passionately, you motivate people to act with energy and purpose, bringing them together to work towards common goals and the bigger picture.

Live with purpose

Great leaders live each day with intention and purpose, and inspire others to do the same. Purpose is a sense of knowing that your life has meaning, value and importance. Living with purpose makes a positive impact and inspires those around you.

Purpose not only gives our lives meaning but also moves us from 'what we do' to 'why we do it'. Purpose is the reason you show up each day.

Build others up

True leaders do not inspire and create more followers; they inspire and create future leaders.

They do this by building and lifting others up and helping them reach their full potential. They encourage them to share their ideas, acknowledge their efforts and contribution and provide them with opportunities to grow. Building others up not only inspires individuals, but also builds strong teams.

When you help others succeed, you will succeed!

Create stretch goals

Stretch goals inspire us to realise our unlimited possibilities and push us beyond where we think we can go. Stretch goals can be implemented in both our professional and personal lives. They encourage us to think outside the box and explore new ideas and strategies.

Stretch goals often push us beyond our comfort zones, and this is where growth happens. No-one ever grew being comfortable.

Work with your people

Inspiring leaders are highly collaborative. They work alongside their people, offering support – rather than telling people what to do. Working together with your people can unleash energy that boosts creativity, productivity, engagement, communication and trust.

Working with your people moves you from 'me' to 'we'.

Invest in your people

When we invest in our people, we are telling them that we believe in them and they are worthy. We inspire them to be the best they can be.

Investing in our people brings multiple benefits: they become more engaged, they are learning and growing, staff turnover is reduced, culture improves, future leaders are developed and loyalty is built. This not only benefits the individual, but also means organisations prosper.

Be fearless

Fearless leaders inspire others to become more fearless. They open others' minds up to new possibilities and help people believe the impossible is possible. They are energetic, passionate, resilient and bold, and have self-belief.

It is this fearlessness that allows leaders to be vulnerable, embrace their own failure and weaknesses, learn from their mistakes and try again.

Fearlessness means always doing what is right, not what is easy or popular.

Take action

People are inspired by what people do, not what they say. Actions speak louder than words. When a leader is all talk and no action, their words become empty and meaningless.

Leaders can have great ideas but unless they are actioned they remain just that – ideas. Taking action produces results and builds relationships, trust and reputation.

INFLUENCE

Great leadership is influence, not authority.

Influence typically means to affect or change someone. Great leaders do this in a positive way, helping their people become better versions of themselves today than they were yesterday.

Influence can have an effect on a person's character and development, the way they behave and even the way they see the world.

When someone makes an impression on us, good or bad, we remember them for how they influenced us.

We can positively influence those around us by:

- ✧ believing in our people
- ✧ building trust
- ✧ being consistent
- ✧ being assertive, not aggressive
- ✧ giving of ourselves
- ✧ being personable
- ✧ giving our people a voice
- ✧ investing in others' success.

Believe in your people

There is no greater empowerment and support you can give someone than to look them in the eye and say, with sincerity and conviction, 'I believe in you.' When you believe in someone, it helps them to find an inner strength they didn't know they had. It strengthens them emotionally, intellectually and spiritually.

When you believe in someone, you inspire them to achieve their potential and even sometimes the impossible.

Build trust

Influence is most often and most easily built through trust. Only when you are a trusted leader will people be open to your influence.

Trust is the foundation that must first be built if you want to create healthy and influential working environments and relationships. The easiest way to build trust is through open and honest communication.

Be consistent

When you execute a consistent style of leadership, set consistent expectations, give consistent rewards and are consistent in your behaviours, people see you as someone they can rely on.

Consistency is vital for building influence and trust. If you're consistently motivated by your values and principles, people will be more inclined to follow you, buy into your ideas and back you up. Inconsistency is the fastest way to ruin your reputation.

Be assertive, not aggressive

Assertive leaders present their thoughts and ideas with confidence, conviction and self-belief, in a way that influences others. Being assertive means expressing yourself in an open, honest way; it's being authentic in the way you communicate your values, opinions and feelings.

Aggressive behaviour is emotionally charged, lacks consideration and empathy for others and often ends in insult. This is not the way to influence others.

Give of yourself

Leaders give of themselves constantly, whether it's time, knowledge, energy, support, motivation or insights. The more leaders give of themselves, the more success those around them will achieve.

Remember, leaders set the tone for how organisations behave so when the leader gives, people also want to give back. When a leader values her team and shows appreciation, people go above and beyond. Grateful leaders build loyal teams.

Be personable

Great leaders are personable, approachable and human.

Personable leaders give and expect trust, value others' efforts and are open with praise and recognition. They have great people skills and seek to find the best in others. They influence through authentic and deep connections.

Being personable is about asking questions, making time for others and being truly present. It is also important when cultivating team camaraderie.

Personable leaders make others feel important.

Give your people a voice

Give everyone a voice. Great ideas don't just come from the top. Create an environment where every level of the organisation is encouraged to speak up and have a voice. When people know their voice is heard they are more open to sharing ideas, knowledge and skills.

People will feel more confident to communicate their views and influence matters that affect the organisation and themselves when they know their voice will be listened to. Take time to respect and acknowledge everybody's opinion.

Giving others a voice also builds open and trusting relationships, which can contribute to organisational success.

Invest in others' success

True leaders bring out the personal best in those around them and celebrate that success.

Recognising and celebrating success is a very powerful motivator for individuals and teams because it reinforces the meaning behind all of their hard work, and it shows appreciation for the achievements. When people have success, this builds confidence and allows them to strive for bigger and better and to take the next step towards achieving the next goal.

IMPACT

Impact means being someone people remember – through our actions, through our words, through our confidence, through our kindness and through our ability to influence and inspire.

It is about using the resources available to us – regardless of our position or wealth –to have a lasting and positive impact on ourselves and our family, friends, colleagues, organisations and society. Leadership is not about authority; it is about the courage to be different and the willingness to lift others up and make a positive impact on those around us.

Leadership affects our everyday interactions and experiences. As leaders in our own lives, everything we say and do has an impact on us and those around us.

We can positively have an impact on those around us by:

- giving back
- being a mentor
- staying positive
- inviting conversation
- allowing others to shine
- backing our people
- listening
- being a coach.

Give back

When we give back, we create a ripple effect that goes far beyond those we help. You may be in a position to help others who are not as fortunate as you – perhaps through generous gifting or by giving your time or love.

We all have something to give. Even small gestures can create an impact and encourage others to be kinder, more forgiving and more willing to lend a helping hand.

Be a mentor

Being someone's mentor is a fantastic opportunity to make an impact. Working with someone as their mentor allows you to guide, support, challenge, inspire and develop another person's skills. Anyone can be a mentor because we are all great at something. You may even share different skills with several mentees.

As a mentor, you get to help less experienced people in areas you are knowledgeable and passionate about. By being a mentor to someone, you can have an everlasting impact on their future.

Stay positive

Great leaders stay positive. They handle crises and challenges with confidence and calmness, and inspire others to do the same.

A positive leader will look at each situation as an opportunity to learn and improve and to find new ways of doing things. They have the ability to immediately transform negativity with their optimistic enthusiasm and inspire those around them.

Invite conversation

Great leaders invite conversation. You might not even know the skills your smart and talented team members possess if you don't make the time to talk to them.

In meetings, encourage conversation, different ways of thinking and new ideas, and be enthusiastic about what your people have to say. A leader's job is not only to inspire others but also to create an environment where people inspire each other through conversion and action.

Allow others to shine

Great leaders allow others to shine. Instead of taking all the credit, a great leader will always pass the credit onto others. I have always believed in a team effort. Praise others for a job well done – for a project completed, a pitch won or a mission accomplished.

By publicly shining the light on others, calling out their accomplishments and acknowledging their commitment, you'll inspire them to work harder and continually strive for improvement.

Back your people

Great leaders back their teams no matter what. You are called a leader for a reason: you lead through good times and bad; you protect, nurture, encourage and pick your people up when they fall over.

Your team looks to you for guidance and support. It is your responsibility to care for them. This can have a huge impact on your team members feeling confident taking risks and trying new things, because they know their leader has their back.

When leaders look after their people, people look after their leader.

Listen

When we think about the most important qualities of great leaders, we might think of being able to inspire others, the ability to delegate and having great problem-solving skills. All of these qualities are signs of a great leader, but one of the most effective ways to have an impact on someone is simply listening to them.

The difference between a good leader and a great leader is the ability to truly listen and value other people's opinions, ideas and perspectives. Remember: when you are talking, you are not listening.

Be a coach

Coaching is something every leader must do. It can be done one-on-one or in a group situation, depending on the coaching requirement. One-on-one coaching with a team member is a great way to review their progress, acknowledge their achievements, offer direction and guidance and set goals.

Coaching your people allows you to have focused and intentional conversations to build on their skills and talents. It helps them grow in confidence and competence, which then motivates and inspires them to take action and reach their full potential.

—

I asked some inspirational women what their greatest leadership lesson was. Their fascinating answers are recorded overleaf.

Take risks and fight for what you believe in

'On a leadership immersion program in India a number of years ago, I witnessed the most meaningful moment of leadership in my life. I sat in a small room on a dirt floor in a tiny village called Lahora, three hours out of Jaipur in Rajasthan. I was talking to a woman named Badam Devi, the elected *sarpanch* (village leader) – an illiterate agricultural worker from a marginalised community who lowered her veil when she spoke. Yet against all odds – including chronic corruption within the bureaucracy as well as centuries-old patriarchy and gender inequality – Badam Devi had managed to have roads built in her community for access and safety, pensions for widows who were otherwise denied them, schools built and kids fed at school (so they would at least have one meal a day). She had a vision for her community. She had built a succession plan for her tenure through (what we would call) sponsorship of younger women in her village. She was courageous and determined, and she had fellowship like nothing I had ever witnessed. She took risks and fought hard for the rights of women and girls in her community. I was witnessing the rawest but most effective form of leadership I have ever encountered. I will never forget her, and think of Badam Devi often as I navigate my own leadership journey.'

Olivia Ruello – CEO, Business Chicks

Lead well when the going gets tough

'Throughout my career the most important leadership learning is that great leaders are those who perform when the going gets tough, not just when things are going well. It's very easy to be an effective and popular leader when times are good, the economy is booming and all the stars are aligned. However, when things don't go to plan, when there is a lack of direction, when the team has lost confidence or when external factors throw you into chaos, this is when true leadership is tested. A great leader creates calm, builds confidence, gives hope, provides clarity and direction and always has your back in times of adversity. This is true leadership.'

Lisa Furnari – Retail Manager

Look to your own behaviour first

'One of my greatest lessons in leadership came with a good deal of pain but lifelong benefits ever since. As a CEO, I had a management team. One of those managers was always outsmarting me, stealing my limelight and making out that I wasn't across the detail by creating the detail for me. She was well respected, well liked and seen as competent and caring by her peers and subordinates – but I saw through it all. She was controlling, wanting to be "the best" and "first" and "liked". Then, I faced my demons and did some personal growth. I experienced the pain of shame when I realised my glasses were coloured "self-absorbed". I recall the relief on her face as I thanked her for the way she had tried her best to support me, think for me, achieve for me and represent me in her every action. The lesson I learnt: we interpret the behaviours of others through a loaded perspective of self.'

Helen Treloar – leadership passionista

Encourage your team to trust themselves

'I have experienced so many meaningful moments of great leadership that I feel incredibly lucky; from my father constantly reminding me throughout my childhood (and still to this day!) that I can do anything I put my mind to, to a boss who trusted me so implicitly he financed the launch of not just one but two of my dream magazines. But one moment that particularly stands out, probably because it was a turning point in my career, was with my very first editor. I had mustered up the courage to ask for a promotion, and after pleading my case, she nodded and then said perilously: "On your own head be it." Those six little words, terrifying and motivating in equal measure, instilled in me the importance of responsibility and determination, and of trusting my vision, instinct and abilities. They've probably, in some way, made me into the leader I am today.'

Susan Armstrong – Content Director, The CEO Magazine

Knowing yourself is the beginning of all wisdom.

ARISTOTLE

SIX PRINCIPLES OF GREAT LEADERSHIP

Having worked with many different leaders during my 30-year career, I've learnt that there is definitely no 'one size fits all' answer to great leadership.

We can all be **leaders by design** and choose our unique formula for success. We can intentionally become the leaders we wish to be, and decide how to live our lives through leadership.

That said, there are some attributes that I have found many great leaders have in common. Let's take a look.

1. You know yourself

Great leadership begins with the person, not the position.

What makes you tick? What gets you going? What are you good at? What are you bad at? When you really know yourself, this creates a platform on which great leadership can be built.

Before you can lead others, you must first know yourself. Knowing yourself is the foundation of strong character, purpose and authenticity. It's only when you understand who you are – not who the world thinks you are – that you're ready to lead. Knowing who you are requires you to understand your strengths, weaknesses, values, beliefs, motivations and desires.

Ask yourself...

What do you really know to be true about yourself? What are three to five of your biggest strengths?

_____

_____

_____

_____

_____

What are three to five things about yourself that you consider to be your weaknesses?

_____

_____

_____

_____

_____

In your day-to-day job, which areas or tasks do you really thrive in?

_____

_____

_____

And which areas could you improve upon for better outcomes?

_____

_____

_____

2. You have strong values

When your values are clear, making decisions becomes much easier.

Great leaders have strong values that guide not only their teams and organisations, but also their everyday lives.

Values are what's most important to us; they are the fundamental beliefs of a person or organisation. These values dictate behaviour, guide and motivate our attitude and actions, support our decision-making, and can help us understand the difference between right and wrong.

If you want to be a leader people will choose to follow, you must demonstrate your values every day rather than just say you have them.

> One of my core values is to
> help redefine what it means to be a
> strong and beautiful woman in the
> music and fashion worlds, and
> to empower the wonderful things
> that make us unique.

JANELLE MONÁE

I'll share more about values a little later in the book – but until then, here are a few thought-starters.

Ask yourself...

What are your most important values? Remember, these are the things that are most important to *you* personally.

_____

_____

_____

_____

In which ways do your values come through when you are leading others (at home and at work)?

_____

_____

_____

_____

How do you react when your values are challenged?

_____

_____

_____

_____

Can you think of an example in your daily life that demonstrates the way you live according to your values?

_____

_____

_____

_____

3. You have a clear vision

A great leader creates an inspiring vision of the future, motivates people to engage with that vision and supports them in achieving it.

A clear vision is essential for focusing your attention on what matters most – whether that be in business or in life.

> ## Greatness starts with a clear vision of the future.
>
> SIMON SINEK

When leaders clearly and passionately communicate their vision, this can motivate people to act with passion and purpose, and help ensure everyone is working towards a common goal.

A vision takes into consideration the past, present and future. It represents who you are as a person and leader and what you stand for. It can even embody the legacy you want to leave behind. It can be a picture or an idea you have in your mind of yourself, your relationship, your business, or anything you want to happen in the future.

Vision is about seeing the bigger picture. It enables you to see beyond what's possible today and look towards what is possible in the future.

Although a vision is important, remember that people follow the leader first and the vision second. If people are not committed to you, they will not be committed to your vision – no matter how well you communicate it.

Ask yourself...

Do you have a clear vision for your career, your team, your home life, your relationships and/or your family?

_____

_____

_____

_____

_____

_____

What problem is your vision trying to solve?

_____

_____

_____

_____

Who is going to benefit from you achieving your vision, and why?

_____

_____

_____

_____

What do you need to do/make/enable for this vision to come true?

_____

_____

_____

_____

4. You lead with courage

Courage comes from the Latin word 'cor', which means heart. It takes great courage and strength of heart to be a great leader.

Courage is the most important of all these principles, because without courage we can't practise any other principle consistently. Courage is that 'x factor' that I believe distinguishes great leaders from mediocre ones. Courageous leaders are willing to climb over obstacles, take risks, walk into the darkness, do what's difficult and sometimes even attempt the seemingly impossible. Courage is not the absence of fear, but rather the ability to overcome fear when we want something bad enough for ourselves and others.

A courageous leader forges a path forward and inspires others to follow. They lead by example and have the difficult conversations. They don't walk away when things get tough. They give everyone the confidence to believe in themselves and their abilities.

Courageous leaders are what we need in the new era of leadership. They are the people every employee hopes to report to and every organisation should aspire to hire.

> Courage doesn't always roar.
> Sometimes courage is the quiet voice
> at the end of the day saying,
> 'I will try again tomorrow'.
>
> MARY ANNE RADMACHER

Do you have the courage to do things you never thought you could do, to climb mountains you never thought you could climb and achieve things bigger than you have before?

Ask yourself ...

What is stopping you from being courageous?

_____

_____

_____

_____

_____

What are you most afraid of?

_____

_____

_____

_____

What do you wish you had the courage to do – at work or in your personal life?

_____

_____

_____

_____

In three years from now, what will you regret if you don't have the courage to take action on it today?

_____

_____

_____

_____

5. You give to others

Great leaders not only go first, but also give first.

When we think about giving, our thoughts often automatically turn to *gifting* – whether that is money or tangible gifts. When we think about it in the context of leadership, there are other gifts that don't have a monetary value, but have value beyond a price tag.

You could give someone:

- an opportunity
- the benefit of the doubt
- your time
- praise for a job well done
- permission to make a mistake
- feedback
- a little extra support.

These acts of giving reflect generosity of spirit – a quality most admired in great leaders.

> Since you get more joy out of
> giving joy to others, you should put
> a good deal of thought into the
> happiness that you are able to give.
>
> ELEANOR ROOSEVELT

Giving is about being in service to others. Leadership is not about the number of people who serve you; it is about the number of people you serve.

Ask yourself...

What are some of the gifts you give to others?

_____

_____

_____

_____

As a leader, how can you better serve others?

_____

_____

_____

_____

How much of what you do serves yourself? How much is for other people?

_____

_____

_____

_____

_____

When was the last time you served someone at great cost to yourself?

_____

_____

_____

_____

6. You lead by example

Great leaders influence their people by setting a good example. Actions speak louder than words.

Leading by example is about leaders setting the tone. They act in a way that shows others how to act. They must be good role models and walk the walk if they want people to follow.

If leaders want to inspire and empower their people a 'do as I say, not as I do' leadership style is not going to cut it. This will make people resentful, disengage and have little or no respect for their leader.

> The reality is that the only way change comes is when you lead by example.
>
> ANNE WOJCICKI

I have always tried to lead by example and would never ask anything of my team that I was not prepared to do myself.

Leaders who lead by example make it easier for others to follow them.

Ask yourself...

In what ways do you already lead by example – positively or negatively – at work and at home?

_____

_____

_____

_____

_____

_____

What are some things you could do to ensure your actions are aligned with your words?

_____

_____

_____

_____

_____

_____

Think of a leader you admire; what are some of the ways they powerfully lead by example?

_____

_____

_____

_____

_____

Leadership

Empowerment

Accountability

Dedication

Engagement

Resilience

Support

Honesty

Integrity

Passion

Six

THE POWER OF KINDNESS

I refuse to believe that you cannot be both compassionate and strong.

JACINDA ARDERN

Kindness isn't the first word that comes to mind when you think about great leadership, right?

Well, I'm here to challenge that. I strongly believe that leading with kindness is what will separate good leaders from great leaders of the future.

I'm not just talking about leadership at the CEO level, either – I'm referring to leadership at all levels of your life: in your work, with your family, in your community and in your place of worship.

I believe that kindness is the new leadership superpower – it's a new and powerful currency that can be traded for high performance and strong results.

You may have heard of – or worse, experienced firsthand – situations of bullying, intimidation or dealing with difficult people in the workplace. This kind of behaviour can be very destructive to both people and organisations. Unfortunately, these are issues that have been around for a long time and will only continue unless leaders step up and start leading with kindness and compassion.

The old era of leadership was about status, title, power, dictatorship and having people do what you say.

The new era of leadership is about kindness, compassion, authenticity, collaboration and trust – and being a leader people choose to follow.

Kindness is defined as the quality of being friendly, generous and considerate. Affection, gentleness, warmth, concern and care are words that are associated with kindness.

It's a common misconception that being a kind leader makes you a weak leader. I believe that being a kind leader requires courage and strength. Kind leaders are very capable of making good and strong business decisions – even tough decisions with kindness.

Kind leadership brings in all the different elements of authenticity, transparency, warmth, trust and empowerment. When we talk about kind leadership, what we really mean is including a little of each of these different attributes in your day-to-day leadership.

I believe it's time for kind leaders to step up and have a voice and be the game changers for our generation and future generations. We may not be able to change the past, but we can shape the future.

It's time to shine the spotlight on leading with kindness in every aspect of our lives.

> ## The qualities I most admire in women are confidence and kindness.
>
> OSCAR DE LA RENTA

KINDNESS FROM THE TOP

Kindness is one of my values and is right up at the top of my priority list when it comes to the way I lead.

I believe one of the greatest gifts we can give another is kindness. Being a kind leader is essential in today's world and in my experience it leads to happier, more collaborative and more productive teams.

As a leader, I have always made time to get to know my people and support them to reach their goals. I've created places where people love to come to work each day.

I do this because I genuinely care for people. I have always strongly believed that if you take care of your people, your people will take care of you and your business. People are the heartbeat and success of any organisation, and it's essential that we treat them accordingly.

In my role as CEO, I wanted to know everyone at every level of the organisation. Hierarchy never mattered to me; people did.

Every person who joined our head office would sit with not only the heads of each department for an induction, but also me personally for a company overview and a 'get to know you' session.

I would share a little bit about myself and my leadership style and my expectations with them, along with explaining the company's strategy and values. I'd spend time finding out about them and what made them tick personally and professionally, as well as learning from their experience and knowledge. I always wanted people to feel bigger than just the seat they sat in.

New people bring new thinking. I have never understood the practice of inducting people by giving them a copy of their job description, showing them their desk, telling them what to do and when to do it, and asking them to conform with the way the organisation thinks and operates. This style of leadership is against everything I stand for. I have always seen new people as a new set of eyes, with new ideas and fresh thinking. When people are given the opportunity to share ideas and experiences, they feel valued – and they do amazing things.

In this new era of leadership, the organisations that thrive will be those that cultivate a culture of openness, mentoring, trust, inclusivity, kindness and empowerment for their people.

Of course, not all women have the same leadership style but generally women bring to leadership a range of qualities modern leaders need in today's world: authenticity, transparency, self-awareness, warmth and emotional intelligence.

A huge part of being a great leader is understanding and valuing the people you lead. It's about embracing the different personalities you work with and creating a culture that encourages individuals to bring their best selves to work each day. Employees want more consistent feedback, delivered with kindness; they want to build trust within their peer group, develop meaningful relationships and have a better life in balance.

My role as a leader has always been to create a 'circle of trust' for my people. A circle of trust is a space where people feel safe; it means that people feel confident to speak up, challenge the status quo and bring new thinking and ideas to the table. It means that when you fall over, you know someone will be there to help you pick yourself back up. It means looking after the people to the left and right of you. It also means having clear expectations, setting boundaries and providing honest, open feedback.

When leaders create a circle of trust, people feel supported, more connected and more fulfilled at work. They contribute more of themselves and will always work harder to see that the leader's vision is advanced.

Great leaders don't have one persona at home and a different one at work; they bring their whole, authentic selves to work. They nurture, mentor and support their people.

You can see how this concept can apply to many areas of your life: at work, in your relationships, with your children and within your community. Being a leader isn't just about how you 'manage staff'; if you're a parent, you're leading tiny humans every day. If you work alongside others, you have the opportunity to model kind behaviour. If you are a partner, you can bring love and compassion to another.

WHY LEAD WITH KINDNESS?

Kindness may be one of the least acknowledged and appreciated leadership qualities, and that needs to change.

Kindness has so many benefits – not only to the receiver, but also to the giver, whether that's in organisations or just in our day-to-day lives. In my experience, organisations that value kindness have higher employee engagement, lower turnover of their teams and higher productivity.

Kindness empowers others to lead with positivity, purpose and an open mind. This encourages new ideas, innovation and collaboration.

If leaders show kindness, they accelerate trust and in turn create happier, more empowered employees who will be inspired to share and deliver on the organisation's goals and vision.

Leading with kindness can encourage and facilitate:

- engagement
- motivation
- employee retention
- innovation and creativity
- trust
- meaningful relationships
- confidence
- improved performance.

I've always loved this quote from William Baker and Michael O'Malley's book *Leading with Kindness*:

> *In order for companies to improve, the people of the organisation have to become smarter and more resourceful and work together more effectively over time. For this to work, people have to care about their work, the company and one another. This requires the expert orchestration of a kind leader.*

In other words, kind leadership also means good business. Kindness has been proven to have an impact on people's happiness, and happier people are 12 per cent more productive, according to a study by Warwick University. 'Happier workers use the time they have more effectively,' the study claims, 'increasing the pace at which they can work without sacrificing quality.'

I walk in front
when I need to lead,
I walk behind
when I need to push
and I walk by your side
when you need a hand to hold,
letting you know that we
are all in this together.

COLLEEN CALLANDER

UNLOCKING KINDNESS IN LEADERSHIP

Kindness is contagious. A single act of kindness often starts a ripple effect, as others embrace positivity and share kindness themselves.

Kindness can be contagious not only in your organisation but also in your community, relationships and home.

Ask yourself ...

Consider an area of your life in which you lead: at work or in your personal life. What does kind leadership mean to you?

_____

_____

_____

How do you see kind leadership playing out in others and how do you enact it yourself?

_____

_____

_____

What changes would you like to see happen in your workplace or home to encourage kind leadership?

_____

_____

_____

What small changes could you make to contribute to a kinder environment, at work or at play?

_____

_____

FIVE THINGS KIND LEADERS HAVE IN COMMON

1. Kind leaders treat people like people

Kind leaders recognise that people are people, not machines.

Machines have serial numbers.
People have names.

During my years as CEO, I made a habit of walking through my office building most mornings to say hello to my team, always using their first name.

I remember a team member once saying to my assistant, 'I can't believe that the CEO remembers my name... I'm no-one.' And my assistant replied, 'Everyone is someone to Col.'

My door was always open and I valued every single person's contribution. I often think back to my early days in retail when I worked as a sales assistant and senior management would visit our store. It would be a huge deal, with much preparation and excitement in anticipation of their visit.

During one of these visits, the senior management team arrived and not one of them spoke to me or any of the other team members – they only spoke to the store manager. I remember how that made me feel: small, undervalued and unappreciated.

I made myself a promise from that day forward that no-one would ever be invisible to me when I rose up the ranks. To this day, whenever I have visited a store, I have made sure I introduced myself to every single person and asked them their name.

Ask yourself ...

Have you ever experienced a time when you felt like you were invisible or undervalued? How did that make you feel?

_____

_____

_____

_____

_____

_____

When was the last time you made an effort to treat someone like a real person and with kindness, when there was no material benefit to you to do so?

_____

_____

_____

_____

_____

_____

When we treat people like people, rather than just a number, why do you think this has such a positive impact?

_____

_____

_____

_____

_____

2. Kind leaders set clear expectations

We have all heard the saying, 'It's not about the destination, it's about the journey'. Well, in my opinion, both are true.

We are all on a journey – whether that be in our relationships, careers or personal lives. We all encounter lessons along the road through hardship, discovery, heartache, failure, joy, success, celebration, difficulties and sometimes even danger.

The role of a leader is to support that journey, while at the same time communicating a clear destination.

People will never deliver on the leader's expectations if those expectations are not clear in the first place. Clear expectations help set people up for success. In my experience, failure occurs as a result of unclear expectations far too often.

Watching people grow can be so rewarding, whether you are a leader at work, a parent or a coach. I believe every human has potential, and it is our job as leaders to create environments that allow people to shine – and this starts with providing clear expectations.

Clarity of goals and objectives is essential for success. It gives your team a path forward, helps them focus on what's important, increases their effectiveness and helps them monitor their progress and continuously grow and improve.

Ask yourself...

What's your destination?

_____

_____

_____

_____

_____

_____

_____

Is your team clear on your expectations?

_____

_____

_____

_____

_____

_____

_____

What do you need to do to give them greater clarity?

_____

_____

_____

_____

_____

_____

_____

3. Kind leaders give honest feedback

The ability to give and receive feedback is an extremely important leadership skill.

Giving honest feedback kindly is a fantastic gift – whether it's negative or positive feedback. Positive feedback encourages people to keep going and strive to be even better. Negative or constructive feedback helps people grow by encouraging them to consider where and how they can improve.

People will only experience feedback as a gift when it is delivered well. Giving honest feedback poorly can destroy a person's self-confidence and demotivate them.

When leaders are not honest with their people it's generally because they don't like confrontation, are uncomfortable with the situation, haven't made their expectations clear, don't know how to give feedback or don't want to hurt the recipient's feelings.

As a kind leader, you must tell people when they're not meeting expectations and, more importantly, why. Remember: you need to have made your expectations clear first and foremost. These sorts of conversations can be tough, but can actually build trust if they are handled with honesty and kindness.

I have always lived by the saying, 'Honesty is the best policy'. I truly believe this. Even after some of the most challenging conversations, people's parting words have often been, 'Thank you for being honest'. As a kind leader, I always stay true to myself and others.

To be a kind leader you have to be honest with yourself as well as being honest with others. Honesty starts with the person in the mirror.

Ask yourself...

How do you generally deliver feedback?

_____

_____

_____

_____

_____

_____

Are you afraid of giving negative feedback? Why?

_____

_____

_____

_____

_____

_____

How could you offer feedback to your team, workmates or even your children in a way that makes them feel supported?

_____

_____

_____

_____

_____

_____

4. Kind leaders encourage growth

Kind leaders are encouragers. They say the words people *need* to hear, not *want* to hear. They not only talk to your head, but also talk to your heart with the encouragement, feedback and inspiration you need to grow.

Kindness doesn't mean always saying things are great and wonderful. Kindness also means challenging your people to be their best, reach their potential, push beyond their comfort zones and care enough to speak the hard truths.

Giving your people more responsibility is a great way to encourage growth. Share with them the attributes and qualities you see in them, and help them see how they can utilise these gifts for self-growth. This also expresses your faith in their ability and cultivates them as future leaders by making them more accountable.

I've always encouraged people to make decisions by saying, 'You've got this... I trust in your ability' or 'You're the expert in your field; I'm backing you' or even 'You've given this great consideration; I know you're going to make the right decision. I have complete faith in you.'

When you allow your people to make decisions, you are encouraging them to lead and feel empowered. Not only does this foster personal growth, but it also lets them know that you believe in them and gives them the opportunity to prove you right.

Always remember to praise and appreciate your people. A little bit of praise goes a long way and encourages people to keep going, keep stretching and keep striving. Let them know how much their great work matters to the organisation, and that they inspire others around them to do better and be better.

I believe in human potential and nothing makes me happier than watching people grow and thrive. Some people take little steps and others giant leaps, and that's okay. Even the smallest step forward is a step in the right direction.

Most people want to do a little better tomorrow than they did today, and it is the leader's role to support others' hopes and dreams.

Ask yourself ...

What words do you use or could you use to encourage those around you?
This can be in any part of your life, personal or professional.

_____

_____

_____

_____

_____

_____

Do you allow others to make decisions as a part of their growth? If not,
why? What can you do to change that?

_____

_____

_____

_____

_____

_____

When you have encouraged others around you, what positive changes
have you noticed?

_____

_____

_____

_____

_____

5. Kind leaders build human connection

Some of the best leaders I have ever met or worked with are those who build real human connections that are about the whole person and go beyond a role or job title.

A connected leader is someone with high self-awareness who comes across as a human being and is not afraid to be vulnerable.

When you build human connections, people feel that you genuinely care. They will connect with you as a leader on a much deeper level and give you their undivided loyalty and support.

Building human connections also builds the trust needed to freely discuss ideas, problem solve, increase efficiencies, collaborate and, most importantly, support each other.

When there is low human connection within an organisation, there will also be low levels of innovation and creativity, along with silo behaviour driving little or no collaboration. It also leads to people looking out for themselves and even finger pointing, especially when the going gets tough.

When you lead with kindness, you encourage human connection. Connected leaders use compassion, kindness, empathy and trust to not only build their tribe, but also help them grow, thrive and succeed.

The time for kindness is now.

I asked some inspirational women what kindness in leadership meant to them. You'll love their answers on pages 134–135.

Ask yourself ...

To be more connected, what are some of the qualities you need to work on yourself?

_____

_____

_____

_____

_____

When building human connections, you need to look beyond the person's job role and title to really get to know the real person. How can you do this?

_____

_____

_____

_____

_____

What outcomes might you achieve by becoming more connected?

_____

_____

_____

_____

_____

_____

A kind leader guides, empowers and celebrates

'Kind leadership is inclusive, transparent, authentic and strong, and comes with a deep level of care. Kindness in leadership has a depth to it that builds trust, confidence, character and growth in others, which breeds respect, trust and results. When staff, family and friends are under the care of a kind leader who guides, empowers and celebrates, the ripple effect of happiness, belief in self and personal growth flows into all areas of that person's life. Kindness in leadership is a deliberate and intentional style chosen by those who want to make an impact both personally and professionally on both the results of the company and the people they are leading.'

Shannah Kennedy – Executive life coach, speaker and author

Expect, accept and support failure

'Kindness in leadership to me means creating an environment where you expect, accept and support failure. I'm a firm believer that you can't grow professionally while shielded in bubble wrap. As a leader, I believe you need to give your people the confidence to get back up and go again and humanise setbacks. Encourage resilience and let them know that failure rarely defines someone for the worse; it often only makes you better.'

Sarah Bolitho – Director, Assistance Sydney

Kindness should not be mistaken as weakness

'In my career as journalist, editor and publisher, I have
been privileged to work under a female leadership structure.
To me, kindness from women in leadership is not to be mistaken
with weakness. It is fair in praise, firm when required and brave
under all circumstances. A leader to me is the sum of many
parts of one united vision.'

Assia Benmedjdoub – Editor, Ragtrader

It made me question myself

'Early in the developmental stage of my career, I worked under a
leader who had a tendency to focus on what I did wrong rather than
what I did right – destructive criticism rather than constructive
criticism. I found this leadership style very disempowering and it made
me question myself. From this experience, I learnt the importance of
building and fostering positive relationships by leading first with my
attitude, as this is adopted and reflected by those you work with and
offer leadership to. Through encouragement and positive professional
development, I believe you empower people to achieve their full
potential and thrive in their role.'

Abbey Thomas – Global PR Manager, WelleCo

Deep human connection is...
the purpose and the result of
meaningful life – and it will inspire
the most amazing acts of love,
generosity, and humanity.

MELINDA GATES

Seven

THE POWER
OF SELF

*Whatever
the mind can
conceive and believe,
it can achieve.*

NAPOLEON HILL

The power of self: what does that even mean? In essence, it all starts with *you* believing in *you*.

It's about believing that you can do and achieve anything you put your mind to, eliminating any doubt from your mind, and then having the courage to actually go for those goals.

If you can get your mindset around this, you truly can do anything.

There's no question that when life gets chaotic, the thing we sacrifice the quickest is ourselves – with our health and wellbeing often suffering the worst.

To harness the power of self, first of all you have to make a commitment to yourself that *you* are the priority. It's easy for us, especially as women, to put others before ourselves; to get weighed down by commitments and to keep adding more and more to our plates, even when they're already overflowing. Perpetual overcommitting can very quickly create a life that is out of balance; this leads to stress, anxiety, exhaustion and even burnout.

In the earlier days of my career I was a workaholic – a badge I no longer aspire to own – but I learnt the hard way that it was not a healthy way to live.

I was always the first to the office and the last to leave. I worked ridiculously long hours, getting up in the dark and home in the dark each day. This was what I thought working hard looked like: giving everything you've got, and then 10 per cent more.

Now, I have never been one to shy away from hard work and I still don't, but what I learnt the hard way is that it's essential for me to work smarter, not harder; put boundaries in place; and include self-care in my world. These three things truly were the secret to me clawing my way out of burnout. They allowed me to create a lifestyle where I could be a high-achieving leader who reaches her goals, without sacrificing myself along the way. Let's take a look at how they work.

WORKING SMARTER

I am not a huge fan of the term 'work–life balance'; I much prefer to think about it as having a 'life in balance'. Why do we have to put life into two boxes – one being work and the other being life? That's not how it works; life doesn't fit into neat little boxes.

There are many ways we can work smarter so we prioritise the things that truly matter, and let go of the 'busy work' that tangles up our time and leaves us feeling exhausted and depleted.

I encourage the women I mentor to draw a big circle, and then write down all the parts of their life that fit into that 'circle of life' by percentage. These might include those shown in the following figure:

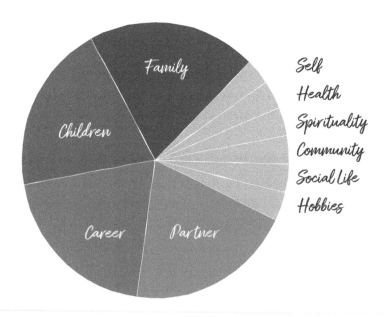

As the graphic depicts, 'self' is often the smallest part of the pie. This was certainly the case in my life when I hit burnout, and it is all too common with the women I work with.

The 80/20 rule

After I came crashing down with burnout, there were many things I had to change in my life. I had to bring some much-needed balance back in. I also needed to add some self-care to my 'circle of life'.

Today, I live by an 80/20 rule for many things in my life. This means that 80 per cent of my life needs to be in balance and 20 per cent can be out of balance or a bit chaotic. I love the 80 per cent balance because it brings calmness, control, routine and happiness to my life; however, on the flip side, I also like the chaotic 20 per cent – it makes me more resilient, strong and grateful. The unexpected nature of chaos can bring different thinking into our lives, allowing us to seize unforeseen opportunities. It teaches us how to adapt, and can often help us clarify what's really important.

When my life isn't in 80/20, I know that means I'm not working very smartly. As the level of chaos creeps up, I start to feel out of balance, out of control, overwhelmed and stressed.

This is when I know I need to take action. I need to change, add or delete something in my life to get back to my happy 80/20 place. Some ideas might be to:

- Change your working hours, if possible and practical.
- Delete the non-essential tasks. (Don't just delegate them, but delete them altogether!)
- Delegate to others those essential tasks that you don't necessarily need to do yourself (and then truly 'let go' and let them do it).
- Create good habits around eating and exercise, such as meal planning and regular movement.
- Block out some time for self-care every day or week.
- Ask for help if and when you need it – such as asking a school mum or a friend to pick up the kids once a week, or for assistance on a work project.

- Say 'no' to social events, invitations or favours that you don't have the time or inclination to commit to.

- Build in boundaries (more on that in a moment).

- Have a 'quit time' each day and resist the temptation to pick up the laptop and go back to work at night.

Your life balance is your responsibility

No-one is going to tell you to slow down or take a load off. No-one is going to make your schedule less busy for you. You have to be good to yourself before you can be good to others.

Always remember: be kind to yourself.

Many people talk about being stressed, overwhelmed or anxious and complain that they don't have a great work–life balance. They think that adding a morning session of yoga a couple of times a week, or doing some meditation, is going to fix everything.

While I encourage adding this kind of self-care into your weekly routine, it's not going to completely fix your work–life balance. You really need to look much deeper than that: pull back some layers and find out what is really causing your life to be out of balance. Only then can you truly make material changes to work smarter, not harder; to prioritise what really matters; and to live your best life in balance.

Start by working out what your 'life in balance' looks like now, and where you would like it to be. Only then can you start shifting the dial to move it towards your perfect life in balance. Earlier I mentioned when my life is in balance it's at 80/20, but you might have a different balance in mind. Don't compare yourself to others; focus on what will work for you and your situation.

Ask yourself ...

What's your happy balance? How much of your life would you like to be set to a routine and in balance, and how much bandwidth do you have for the unexpected?

_____

_____

_____

_____

_____

Are you living with a comfortable and happy sense of balance right now?

_____

_____

_____

_____

_____

If not, what do you need to change, add or delete to get there?

_____

_____

_____

_____

_____

Calendar is key

There are a number of things I can't live without and my calendar is one of them. Call me old fashioned, but I still have a handwritten calendar – something about committing pen to paper, rather than using a digital calendar, works for me. Everything goes in it: work, family, social and health. I like to have a total picture of what each week and month is looking like. Most importantly, in your calendar you need to block out time for yourself to recharge.

Share the load

Delegating is essential if you want to achieve a life in balance. You don't have to do it all and, in fact, you can't. Women are often responsible for the lion's share of household chores, along with our jobs away from home – is it any wonder we sometimes struggle to achieve balance? In the same way that you might delegate at work, you need to do so at home, too. Decide what you must do yourself and what others can take care of. Often, we don't ask for help because we think it means we are failing, or it looks like we are not coping. Other times, we don't ask because we want it done 'right'. Don't be scared to ask for help and don't be fussy about the end result. Many hands make light work – and sometimes 'done' is better than 'perfect'.

Attend to what is most important

Lunch with your partner, work conferences, your kids' school plays, awards nights and networking events – these are all important in their own way, but only you can prioritise what's most important to attend in both your professional and personal life. So many of us have felt trapped between the walls of our obligations and loyalties to others, and then wonder why we feel exhausted and have no time left for ourselves. Be comfortable saying no to the things that don't serve you or your family well. If an event does not align with your goals and values, there's really no need to attend it.

Fill your soul

This is my favourite part of creating a life in balance – it's where all the fun happens. What water, food, air, sleep and sunlight are to your body is what love, acceptance, kindness and balance are to your soul.

Schedule date nights, do something fun with the kids, plan an evening with friends, go away for the weekend, do a digital detox – or just take some time to yourself to watch your favourite old movie, apply a face mask and relax. Balance life's pressures by giving yourself some well-deserved time out doing something that fills your soul, either by yourself or with the people you love.

Set your focus, at work and at home

If you are a working woman, every minute is crucial, at work and home. I make sure I have boundaries around both to maintain my focus. When I am at work there are no personal phone calls (unless urgent, of course). There is no internet banking, no shopping online and no scrolling through Instagram. I am totally focused, and the same applies at home: I have a set time each day where I stop replying to emails and taking phone calls, and I (and my family) become the priority. The more you know yourself and your priorities, the more balanced your life will be and the more content and fulfilled you will feel.

Create a passion project

Making time to do things you actually love and are passionate about is the secret to happiness and maintaining a life in balance. A passion project can also help you learn new skills, meet new people, contribute to your career or maybe even help you find a new one. You get to devote as much or as little time and energy to your passion project as you like... it's yours!

Passion projects nourish our spirit and fill our soul. What is yours?

Boundaries help you...

- ✧ Prioritise your own wellbeing and support a 'life in balance'
- ✧ Make healthy choices and take responsibility for yourself – emotionally, mentally, physically and spiritually
- ✧ Create an equal partnership where responsibility and power are shared
- ✧ Protect your physical and emotional space
- ✧ Stay in control of your life, rather than living in response mode to others
- ✧ Learn how to stand up for yourself and become more assertive
- ✧ Build self-esteem and self-respect
- ✧ Protect the most important person... *you!*
- ✧ Set the basic guidelines of how you want to be treated and how others should behave around you

Think of boundaries as 'no trespassing' signs!

SETTING BOUNDARIES

After I experienced burnout, setting boundaries became hugely important to me. I had been a working mum with very few boundaries all my adult life. I'd barely had any maternity leave – I had four months off with Jake, four months off with Trent and eight months off with Macey – so basically all I had ever known was hard work and long hours in the pursuit of my career.

**If you don't set your own boundaries,
someone else will set them for you.**

Staying true to my boundaries, I had to learn to say 'no' to things that didn't serve me and stop being the pleaser I naturally tend to be. That was hard. I'm sure many of you can relate – saying no when you're a natural people pleaser is about as difficult as it gets!

I had to create two columns. On one side, I wrote things that were 'important to do'. On the other, I listed things that were 'nice to do'.

This is just one way in which I began placing boundaries around my time and energy.

When we find ourselves whining, complaining or feeling like a doormat (this can be at work or in our personal lives), this is often a clear sign we need stronger boundaries.

The fact is: if you don't set your own boundaries, someone else will set them for you – whether they're work colleagues, your boss, your family, your partner or your children. And I promise you, those boundaries won't serve you well, because they haven't been created on your terms!

Ask yourself ...

Do you have good boundaries in place? (Many women I speak to and mentor answer 'no' to this question.)

Think of a few examples where your boundaries are clear and strong, and others where they are a bit wobbly.

Clear boundaries:

_____

_____

_____

_____

_____

_____

_____

Unclear boundaries:

_____

_____

_____

_____

_____

_____

_____

_____

Why you're failing to set clear boundaries

◊ You're not making yourself a priority.

◊ You feel guilty putting yourself first.

◊ You feel like you are being selfish.

◊ You don't like confrontation.

◊ You were never taught how to create healthy boundaries.

Signs you don't have boundaries in place

You feel:

◊ overwhelmed

◊ suffocated

◊ stressed

◊ anxious

◊ depleted

◊ taken for granted

◊ unconfident

◊ resentful.

Blame versus responsibility

You must be in control of setting your own boundaries. When you let others set boundaries for you, you can fall into 'blame' mode rather than taking responsibility for your own life. Let's take a look at the differences between blame and responsibility.

Blame – I never have time for myself to do what I want to do.

Responsibility – I need to take time for me and make my needs a priority.

Blame – I always end up doing everything myself and I am exhausted.

Responsibility – I am tired and overwhelmed and I need to ask for help.

Blame – No-one appreciates the things I do.

Responsibility – I take on way too much, hoping someone will notice and give me praise.

Blame – My work takes up so much of my time, I never have any time for me.

Responsibility – I have chosen to put work first over my own priorities and needs.

If you recognise any of the phrases in the 'blame' category, you might need to shift your thinking towards responsibility. We all need to be in the driver's seat of our own lives.

Five tips for setting boundaries

1. Know your values

Boundaries should be set around the things that really matter, and you can only do this once you are crystal clear on your values and what is most important to you. Creating boundaries around what you value in life and in business supports all of your decision-making and helps you create a life in balance. Only then will you feel content, confident and in control, because the boundaries you set are supporting your values.

2. Communicate clearly

People can't live within your boundaries if they don't know what they are. Being clear and not leaving any grey areas around your boundaries benefits everyone. For example, when I was a CEO, my team members knew that if my office door was open they were welcome to walk in. But if my door was closed, I was off limits and I didn't want any interruptions. This was about putting boundaries around my time to protect me from overload.

3. Don't be afraid to say 'no'

We often say 'yes' more than we say 'no' because we don't want to let people down or disappoint them. Instead, we let *ourselves* down by adding too much to our own plate. We need to start getting comfortable with saying no and being totally okay with it. I am sure you have had many times when you wanted to say 'no' but you couldn't bring yourself to do it, and when it came time to deliver on that commitment you were kicking yourself for saying yes (this has happened to me many times). It's only by saying no that you can concentrate on the things that are really important.

A little story on the power of 'no'

Burnout happens because you're overwhelmed and exhausted – which is often a byproduct of an over-packed schedule. It happens when you've said 'yes' to everything and taken on too much.

We are inundated with requests every day: from our employers, our family, our friends and, perhaps most destructively, ourselves.

Being a person who always wants to please others, I would say 'yes' to everything – even if it came at a great cost to me.

You may not realise it, but you teach people how to treat you. If you say 'yes' all the time, people will keep asking because they know they can also rely on you to do what they need you to do. This is how my schedule ended up so over-stuffed.

Col, can you squeeze in another meeting at the end of the day? *Yes!*

Col, you're invited to another function on Wednesday night, how should I RSVP? *I'll be there!*

Col, can you fly interstate to help with this project? Tomorrow? *Absolutely!*

Col, you have been asked to speak at an event next month, would you like to do it? *Yep, count me in!*

Col, your husband called and asked me to block out this Friday night in the diary as he has a work function and he would like you to join him. You already have a dinner booked in though... *I'll do both!*

While I was really wanting to say 'no' to many of these requests, I would continue to say 'yes' to avoid disappointing anyone. In reality, the only person I was letting down was myself!

An easy way to decide whether the answer should be 'yes' or 'no' is to think about what's really important to you, and what really matters in your life. Do your decisions align with your values, and where you want to invest your time?

Post burnout, I went from feeling uncomfortable saying no to feeling completely fine when the word tumbled out of my mouth. It didn't happen right away; at first, it felt awkward, downright difficult and like I was speaking a foreign language! But once I saw how well it was serving me, my health and my family, I became comfortable with it. Saying no takes practice, but the rewards of putting yourself first are impossible to quantify.

4. **Consider a technology curfew**

   This is a huge boundary that many women I mentor are challenged with. Building in technology boundaries at work and home can be life-changing. You might be surprised to know that some of the smallest changes can be the most effective. For example, no phones at the dinner table; turn off all technology at a certain time; set a time for when you stop replying to emails; no phone next to your bed. Technology is one of the biggest sources of stress and anxiety. Remember: your passion, purpose and dreams are not on your phone.

5. **Prioritise yourself**

   Build a self-care routine and stick to it. The way we start and end our day is super important. Have a morning routine that works for you and fills your soul, whether that means waking up early to go for a walk on the beach, doing some yoga or writing in your journal. Have an end-of-day routine that signals your 'quit time': a shower, a cup of tea, switching off your computer or reading a book. This helps you to unwind, and in my experience makes for a great night's sleep. We serve others better when we serve ourselves and when we don't we can feel undervalued and become resentful.

EMBRACING SELF-CARE

Life is full of commitments, responsibilities and obligations. I get it. We are all leading busy lives and it can become a struggle to fit in time for ourselves when trying to balance everything else in our lives.

One of the most common reasons women give for lack of self-care is, 'I don't have time'. I know, because I used to use this excuse too. I was always too busy!

Busy building my career, busy looking after my family, busy trying to be a good friend and busy trying to be a good sister. I was busy being busy. Don't get me wrong – I *was* genuinely busy, but we should never be too busy to look after our own health and wellbeing and give time to what is important to us.

> **You will always make time for whatever is most important in your life.**

45 to Thrive

I'm now here to challenge the idea that 'I'm too busy' can be a valid excuse. Instead, I hope to change your life with my concept of 45 to Thrive. It changed mine!

Here's the thing: when we tell ourselves we don't have time for something, what we are saying is that it is not important or a priority.

I'm here to tell you that you are important, that you are a priority – in fact, you are *the* most important priority in your life. If you want to be the best version of yourself so that you can be good for others, then you need to start being good to yourself first.

The truth is this: you will always make time for whatever is most important in your life.

- If finishing that project is important, you'll make time for it.
- If eating well is important, you'll make time for it.
- If spending time with someone is important, you'll make time for it.
- If exercising is important, you'll make time for it.
- If creating your side hustle is important, you'll make time for it.
- If going to your child's music concert is important, you'll make time for it.
- If studying is important, you'll make time for it.

Get the picture?

It isn't that you don't have time; it's that you haven't made it important enough to take action.

I want you to start placing importance on your biggest asset: you. I want you to do this by implementing 45 to Thrive.

Think about it like this:

- There are 1440 minutes in every 24 hours.
- The average person sleeps for 8 hours (480 minutes).
- This leaves us with 16 hours (960 minutes).

So, out of your 960 minutes of awake time, I'm asking you to find just 45 minutes in your day to dedicate to *you* – that's 45 to Thrive.

It sounds crazy when we say it like that, right? That in 960 minutes in a day, we can't find 45 minutes for ourselves?

It might be taking a bath with some candles burning and listening to some relaxing music. It might be reading a book in a cosy, comfortable spot in your home. It might be doing a yoga class. It might be meditating as soon as you get up in the morning. It might be going for a run, or it might just be enjoying your morning coffee while writing in your journal.

Finding 45 minutes in your day for you will change your life – and you will thrive.

When we focus entirely on giving to others, we can end up overwhelmed, fatigued, stressed and at times even resentful.

Taking time out to care for ourselves can remind us and others that our needs are also important.

How to build self-care into your life

Practising self-care isn't always easy, but there are many different things you can do to build it into your life. It's about finding the things that work best for you and then structuring them into your regular routine. This will not only improve your health and wellbeing but also help you live a life that empowers you to be that fun, fulfilled, confident and vibrant human you want to share with your partner, your kids, your family, your friends and the world.

Here are my top 10 tips for self-care...

1. **Practise 45 to Thrive**

    Build 45 minutes into each and every day for you to thrive. You have time! You only need to find 45 minutes out of 960 minutes to claim as your own.

2. **Put yourself first**

    Taking care of yourself and putting yourself first is the pathway to fulfilment and to higher performance in life. It may feel uncomfortable at first, but it will be a gift to others in the long run when you are giving them the best of you, because you've taken care of yourself first and foremost.

3. **Get outside**

    Breathe in some fresh air, listen to the waves crash at the beach or sit and listen to the birds singing in the tree. Connecting with nature helps us find peace in our busy lives and makes us happier and improves our mood.

4. **Exercise daily**

    It doesn't matter what it is: walking, tennis, a gym session, pilates or yoga. Daily exercise can help you both physically and mentally. It can boost your mood and energy levels, help with relaxation and sleep quality and reduce stress. Move your body!

5. **Eat well**

    What you eat can have a significant impact on your health, wellbeing and feelings of vitality. Eating well can improve your memory, help to reduce the risk of disease and help you to maintain a healthy weight. Plan your meals for the week ahead and eat a well-balanced diet.

6. **Prioritise sleep**

    Sleep can have a huge effect on how we feel both emotionally and physically. Being well-rested leads to us being able to think more clearly; it can also boost our immune system, and lead to a happier and healthier life.

7. **Indulge in retail therapy**

    Studies have shown that shopping actually causes your brain to release serotonin, which is a chemical that makes you feel good. Treating yourself to something new is a great way to reward yourself. (But spend within your means!)

8. **Unplug**

    Take the time to break away from social media, your phone and your computer. Being constantly connected isn't healthy for your mind, body or spirit. Allow yourself to focus on the beauty of being present and in the moment.

9. **Declutter your life**

    We don't declutter our lives as often as we should because it's hard to find the time. However, when we declutter whatever it is that is crowding our lives, it not only helps us be more productive, happy and calm but also gives us back time.

10. **Balance treating yourself with giving to others**

    Giving is a part of who we are and what we do. However, creating a healthy balance between helping others and caring for yourself is vital. You are no good to yourself or others if you're running on an empty tank, so make sure to replenish it.

Letting go of guilt

Letting go of guilt you feel in any area of your life is like lifting sandbags off your shoulders.

As working mothers, for instance, we often live with guilt – I struggled with it daily, especially when my kids were younger.

Women often ask me, 'Can I be a great mum and have a career and everything in between? Can I really have it all?'

What I've worked out is that 'having it all' means different things to different people. And the answer is, yes, you can – but having it all may not look like what you thought it would.

I spent a lot of time in the 'guilt zone' for being a mother and also wanting a vibrant career. I felt guilty when I couldn't turn up to a school event because I was at a conference. I felt guilty when I was travelling for work and would call home to talk to the boys, who either didn't want to talk to me or cried the entire time I was on the phone. I felt guilty when I got home from work late and I had missed bath time and they were already asleep.

And, sometimes, I just felt guilty for having a career at all. I judged myself and thought I was a bad mum and even, at times, a failure – even though logically I knew I was not.

One day I realised that feeling guilty wasn't serving me or my health, or doing my kids or my career any good, either. So, I gave myself permission to let go of the guilt and started focusing on the positive things about being a career woman and a mum, instead of the negatives.

I changed the story I told myself; instead of feeling weighed down and burdened by all the things I was missing, I focused on the value that being a working mum added to our lives.

I was a much happier and more interesting person for working, to begin with. It gave me interests and passions outside the home and my parental duties. It gave me my own identity and helped to define me outside of motherhood.

I was making an impact on those around me through my leadership and showing other women that it's possible to follow your dreams. My job gave me a sense of self-worth and helped build my confidence.

I loved to work; it fuelled my soul. And I realised: why should I deny myself something that I love doing, that brings me joy and that overflows in a positive way into other areas of my life?

I focused on what was important in my life – what really mattered. And that's when I was able to see everything that I did get to see, do, enjoy and experience.

I always turn up to the things that are important to my kids. As soon as I am aware of an important date for one of the kids, it goes straight in the diary as a priority appointment. Yes, I may have missed the odd sports day or presentation, but, overall, I made it to every school-related event that really mattered to them.

This also means that when I am at work, I am 100 per cent focused and when I am at home with my family, I am 100 per cent focused.

So, if you're struggling to let go of the guilt, my suggestion to you is to change the story you are telling yourself.

Ask yourself ...

What benefits does being a working mum add to your life and to your family? The benefits might be financial, social or even practical.

_____

_____

_____

_____

_____

_____

What beliefs do you have around 'good parenting', and how might these be holding you back? For instance, do you truly believe you can only be a good mum if you're always with your kids, 24/7? Or do you think it fosters resilience and problem-solving skills for them to learn to sometimes live without you being at their beck and call?

_____

_____

_____

_____

_____

Are you happy with your current working setup? If you could change anything about your current 'life in balance' in regards to how you manage work and your kids, what would you change?

_____

_____

_____

_____

BELIEVING IN YOURSELF

Throughout our lives we become conditioned to doubting ourselves. Women especially need to start believing in themselves and, just as importantly, each other. When you overcome self-doubt and fear you will have the confidence to take that first step, to take action and move towards your dreams and goals.

Believing in yourself means believing in your own strength, power, resilience and capabilities. It means believing that you can achieve anything you set your mind to and break through any glass ceiling.

So, get clear on your vision and what it is you want to achieve. It might be getting that next promotion, training to run a marathon, starting a new business or raising money for your favourite charity. Whatever it is, write it down, make a vision board or have a clear picture in your mind of what it is you want.

It is much easier to 'be what we can see' than travel along in the dark.

Encourage yourself,
believe in yourself,
and love yourself.
Never doubt who you are.

STEPHANIE LAHART

My tips for fostering self-belief:

- ✧ Don't underestimate your personal power.

- ✧ Practise positive self-talk.

- ✧ Focus on the journey, not just the destination.

- ✧ Celebrate your accomplishments, big and small.

- ✧ Remember that competence builds confidence.

- ✧ Accept the ups and downs.

- ✧ Learn from your mistakes.

- ✧ Visualise your goals and dreams.

- ✧ Trust yourself.

- ✧ Don't let fear stop you.

CELEBRATING YOUR ACHIEVEMENTS

We can get so caught up in life – whether that's at home, at work or in our personal lives – that we forget to slow down and celebrate our achievements.

We are often so focused on what's next, what we haven't achieved or what we could have done better that we forget to pat ourselves on the back for a job well done.

I was definitely one of those people. Rather than taking a moment to pause and celebrate my achievements, I would strive to be better, push myself harder, set my sights on what was next and keep marching forward.

For someone like myself – a self-confessed achievement junkie – this could sound like a great plan to kick goals and be productive. But this kind of attitude is actually detrimental to our health and wellbeing; it's a recipe for burnout. I know, because it happened to me.

When we stop and celebrate our achievements, it not only gives us an awesome rush of dopamine but also builds our confidence, allows us try new things, gives us motivation to keep going and provides a chance to reflect, correct course if necessary and decide on the next steps. Just as importantly, it allows us to enjoy the journey – which can be just as satisfying and rewarding as getting to the final destination.

So, celebrate it all: celebrate a good hair day, a promotion, the perfect chocolate cake you baked, ticking off your to-do list. Celebrate ending that toxic relationship, getting a new job, graduating. Celebrate the birth of a child, speaking up in the meeting, getting a B on your English exam. Celebrate it all, no matter how big or small the milestone.

<blockquote>
She was powerful, not because
she wasn't scared but because she went
on so strongly, despite the fear.

ATTICUS
</blockquote>

Ask yourself...

What have been some of your accomplishments? Write them down —
big and small — and plan how you can celebrate.

What have you accomplished...

Today?

_____

_____

_____

_____

This week?

_____

_____

_____

_____

This month?

_____

_____

_____

_____

This year?

_____

_____

_____

_____

How to celebrate your achievements

◊ Treat yourself to an experience you wouldn't normally stretch to – for example, visit a fancy restaurant or day spa.

◊ Allow yourself a doona day, stay in your PJs and binge on Netflix.

◊ Share the love. Write a letter or send an email of gratitude to someone who helped you get there.

◊ Buy yourself those shoes you have been wanting for ages.

◊ Book a weekend away – with girlfriends, your partner or even on your own!

◊ Pop a bottle of champagne (or kombucha!) and pour yourself a glass.

◊ Keep a notebook or journal of your weekly achievements.

◊ Support someone else in reaching their goals.

◊ Have a party.

◊ Share your achievement on social media.

◊ Accept and enjoy others' compliments.

You are amazing,
talented, beautiful and unique,
and there is not a day that goes by
that you don't have a
reason to celebrate *you*.
So, do it!

COLLEEN CALLANDER

Eight

THE POWER OF PEOPLE

I always believed that one woman's success can only help another woman's success.

GLORIA VANDERBILT

Now, more than ever, it's crucial for women to support each other. Together we can create change, bring about equality and help women flourish in all aspects of their lives – not just in their careers.

As human beings, we're inspired by other people's stories of adversity, accomplishment, fear and failure. It is through these stories that we connect, learn and grow. That's why it's so important to have role models and mentors in our lives.

There are so many qualities used to determine great role models. Ideally, you'll have several role models in your life, providing inspiration and guidance for each of the different areas you are passionate about.

Lifting women up…
Giving them a voice…
Building confidence…
Encouraging each other to reach our full potential…

These are the ways that we can drive
meaningful and lasting change.

I am always inspired by women supporting women, and it is what I have always tried to do – not only as a CEO, but also in my everyday life.

I also strongly believe the next generation of young women must have strong role models to look up to: women who are changemakers, breaking through glass ceilings in their careers and everyday lives. Having positive, fierce, intelligent, kind women making change in the world sends a message of empowerment, paving the way for the next generation to believe their opportunities are limitless.

As we explore the power of role models and mentors in this chapter, I want you to reflect on the people who have inspired you over the years – as well as those you might look up to today to help guide you forward.

WHO ARE YOUR ROLE MODELS?

A role model can come from anywhere: it may be someone you know, or someone you've never met. She could be world-famous, or someone who lives in your neighbourhood. She might be a rock star, an athlete, a teacher, a community leader, an actor, a coach, a philanthropist or maybe even your mum.

A role model is *any* woman you look up to. She is a woman who makes a difference – whether that's in the little things she does in her everyday life or grand gestures made in the public eye.

Great female role models act as a guide to help us understand who we would like to become in the future.

Growing up as a young girl in the '80s, my role models included Princess Diana, for her strength and kindness; Brooke Shields, for her grace and beauty; and Madonna, because she was bold and fearless. At the time, I didn't describe them as role models; in fact, I probably didn't even know what role models were. I just knew I admired these women and felt inspired by their actions, what they stood for and how they behaved.

I also realised later in life that I had role models much closer to home: my parents. All my life, they have both been a constant source of inspiration and guidance. They showed me that:

- Hard work is the key to success.
- It's important to live according to your values.
- Family is everything.
- Anything is possible.
- I should never give up!

BEING A ROLE MODEL TO OTHERS

Throughout my entire career, I have tried to be a positive role model for those around me – particularly women. When I left the Sussan Group in early 2020, I decided the next step in my career was to continue on this path of inspiring and empowering women to live their best lives. I think it's essential for the next generation of females to have positive role models because I've seen and experienced the impact it can have.

I once worked with a young up-and-coming leader called Cristiana. I recognised her passion and energy early on and she quickly rose through the ranks. Cristiana thanked me recently for the role I played as her mentor early in her career. 'You were the leader I looked up to and an amazing role model, not only for myself but also for everyone around you,' she told me. 'You were the kind of leader I wanted to be. You challenged me, empowered me and taught me the importance of believing in myself and staying true to my values.'

I'm so humbled by comments such as these. They really do give me the drive and purpose to keep doing what I'm doing, which is to encourage women everywhere to lead in their own lives – to have a voice, build their confidence and work actively towards workplace equality. Most importantly, these women will inspire the next generation of women to believe in themselves.

Ultimately, it is human nature to be inspired by other people's success and achievements. When we see other women achieve things or obtain positions that we aspire to, it makes it easier for us to imagine ourselves in those roles. It means we are more likely to put ourselves forward. This is also one of the big reasons we need *more* women in leadership roles and why I want to inspire and empower more women to see that the sky really is the limit...

A good role model...

- ◇ Has strong moral values
- ◇ Behaves ethically and demonstrates honesty
- ◇ Demonstrates commitment to a desired goal
- ◇ Is willing to invest the necessary time and effort to achieve
- ◇ Supports causes close to her heart
- ◇ Has a healthy appreciation of her accomplishments
- ◇ Inspires others through her passion to succeed
- ◇ Is influential through the way she shows respect to others
- ◇ Demonstrates selflessness
- ◇ Inspires others with her optimistic outlook
- ◇ Sees the bright side of challenging or difficult situations

Ask yourself...

Who are your role models...

As a woman?

_____

_____

As a friend, sister or daughter?

_____

_____

As a partner?

_____

_____

_____

As a mother?

_____

_____

As an employee or in your career?

_____

_____

_____

As a leader?

_____

_____

Why is it so important that we create strong female role models for the next generation?

So that they learn to believe in themselves.

So that they strive to become powerful leaders.

So that they are inspired to pursue their dream careers.

So that they know they have a voice.

So that they believe anything is possible.

So that they are independent and strong.

So that they aspire to greatness.

So that they believe they can break through glass ceilings.

So that they, in turn, become strong female role models.

So that they can be change makers.

WHAT CAN WE LEARN FROM OUR ROLE MODELS?

Everyone has a story of a time when they had to overcome adversity. Malala Yousafzai's is at the most extreme end: at the age of 15, she was shot by the Taliban in her home country of Pakistan. She went on to recover and became a powerful advocate for girls' education; she has since published her autobiography and was the world's youngest recipient of the Nobel Peace Prize in 2014.

JK Rowling had her world-famous Harry Potter novels rejected several times by different publishers before going on to become one of the world's most famous authors, and one of the UK's richest women. She proves that anything is possible; you've just gotta keep believing.

These stories remind us that setbacks, adversity and even failure shouldn't prevent us from achieving our goals, living out our dreams or finding success.

When we overcome obstacles, it can help us become stronger, work out what's important and prepare us to deal with future setbacks.

This is one of the advantages of having a role model: they act as a constant source of inspiration. Those who inspire us awaken us to new possibilities; they help us believe anything is possible and inspire us to follow our passion and dreams.

When we lack the confidence or motivation to achieve our goals and dreams, it can be very beneficial to have someone to emulate. We feel inspired by their work, accomplishments, determination and success, which can drive us to achieve success of our own.

> **Those who inspire us stand up for what they believe in and do not waiver on their values or beliefs. They admit their mistakes and build others up.**

Often, they are someone who wants to make positive changes in others' lives or even the world, which inspires us to do the same.

While 'success' means different things to different people, if someone is a role model, it means they have done something that makes them successful in your eyes. Whether they are a celebrity, an athlete, someone you work with or a stay at home mum – this person you look up to has valuable qualities that you admire and can learn from.

For example, your mum might teach you how to be kind, even when others are not so kind to you; an athlete could teach you about discipline; and a celebrity might model behaviour of using status for good.

Sometimes even others' failures can inspire and motivate us. Nobody is perfect – not even the people you look up to. Whether they are a celebrity, a gold medallist, a person of power or a sales assistant – *every* human makes mistakes. Mistakes can make us stronger, more resilient and wiser. The key is for us to learn from our and others' mistakes, and turn them into valuable life lessons.

THE POWER OF PEOPLE BEFORE PROFIT

People are at the heart of everything I do. They always have been.

My leadership style evolved very early in my career. I didn't realise it at the time, but I was very purposefully becoming a leader by design. I wasn't consciously thinking about the end game; I just followed my heart and my instincts, and this led me to become the type of leader I always wanted to be.

People and relationships were always important to me, and I could see the impact that putting people *first* could make.

I have never been a leader who was scared of my team being better, smarter or more skilled than me – in fact, I strived for it. I believed having incredible people around me was one of my biggest advantages as a leader.

Throughout my 30-year career I have met leaders at different levels and from different industries with fear in their eyes – scared of being outdone, outshone or outsmarted. I always saw this as a reflection of their own insecurities.

The power of people is stronger than the people in power.

WAEL GHONIM

Way back in 1991, when I had just been promoted to manage a premium store, I had my first taste of managing a large team. This was a store with a bigger footprint, greater sales targets and more staff.

I was 20 years old, managing a $2 million-plus business. It was during this time that I learnt the power of people – a lesson that has stuck with me throughout my career.

Unconsciously, I was recruiting people like me – like-minded people who were energetic, passionate, hardworking and who loved retail and serving customers just as much as I did. I called my team the 'A team': they were all hungry to succeed, but not at each others' cost. Competitive but not destructive; ambitious but supportive.

Week-on-week, month-on-month, we continued to exceed our sales targets and win competitions and I truly believe this was because we had such a passionate, cohesive, supportive team. My people always went above and beyond. They would do anything for me. They gave me their loyalty and commitment because I showed them respect and gratitude and treated them like people I cared about – just as leaders should.

The following year, I was awarded the most prestigious award within the company, given to one manager in each state for exceptional performance. I was one of 55 managers in the running to receive this award, but I was also one of the *youngest* managers in the company at that time – just 21 years old.

When it was announced that I was the winner for Victoria, I knew that this award was not mine alone: it also belonged to the people in my team. They were the ones who had worked so hard over the past year, and who had also put people at the heart of everything they did – not only with customers, but with each other, too.

As a leader I have always had the philosophy that it is the *performance* of people that leads to the *success* of the organisation.

Prioritising the needs and wellbeing of your people can have a remarkable impact on the organisation and your bottom line.

If your staff are valued, trusted, happy, motivated and driven within the workplace, their output will be far higher than that of those who feel undervalued and undermined.

In this profit-driven world we live in today, it's no surprise that sales, margins, shareholder returns and revenue are at the forefront of most leaders' minds. At the end of the day, profit is essential for all businesses both big and small to keep the doors open and allow for reinvestment and growth. But I want to challenge the traditional business focus we have become accustomed to.

> *People before profit* has always been
> my secret weapon.

I have always aimed to create environments where people get up every day and come to work feeling safe, valued, inspired, empowered and fulfilled, where they really love what they do and feel part of something bigger than just themselves. I believe this has been my secret weapon, and one of the biggest success factors for me as a leader.

Remember in chapter 1 we discovered that only 15 per cent of people worldwide are engaged with their jobs? We can buck that trend by creating inspiring and safe workplaces where people are encouraged to be their best selves. As leaders, this is our job.

How to be a leader for the people

◇ Have an open door policy – for absolutely everyone. Being approachable and accessible is key.

◇ Include all staff in your business performance meetings and strategy presentations – not just the select few in management who are deemed 'worthy'. Everyone in the company needs to know what your goals are and how you're tracking.

◇ Serve as a role model at every level.

◇ Be thoughtful about your new employee induction and meet all your staff personally.

◇ Create an environment of women supporting women – all women, not just the top tier.

WALK THE TALK

Leaders first and foremost need to walk the talk. Most leaders will tell you people matter; but where are people on their list of their priorities?

I remember one evening sitting next to a CEO from another company at a dinner and they said to me, 'Colleen, I have heard wonderful things about you and that you are an incredible leader and one for the people. Our number one priority is profit but, of course, our people are also important.'

I replied, 'My number one priority is people. When we take care of our people, profits follow.'

As I moved up the corporate ladder, this remained my philosophy. I loved people and this was my motivation for growth – with my personal growth also contributing to that of others.

Each promotion I received was an opportunity to influence, nurture, grow, empower and inspire more people... first five people, then 10, then 50 and so on.

Today, as I write this book, my purpose is still the same.

Most leaders structure board meetings and strategy presentations using the traditional format of financials, strategy, marketing plans, the customer and *then* people. Perhaps you have experienced a meeting run like this. I have always started mine the other way around. I begin by exploring why people's work matters and how it connects to the bigger picture. I have always believed that people want to feel that their work is part of something greater.

> **People want to feel connected and
> know that they can contribute more than just
> the role they do or the seat they sit in.**

I remember my first day on the job as CEO. I had only been in my office for 15 minutes when a friendly young man with a big smile turned up at my office door with a trolley and two large boxes.

'Hi Colleen! Welcome. I've got your computer here to set up for you,' he said.

I very kindly told him he could take the computer back to the computer room, as I didn't need one. He cocked his head and looked at me very strangely. Without asking me for a word of explanation, he turned around and pushed his trolley back down the hallway.

I had no need for a computer – I had a fabulous executive assistant. We didn't both need a computer. It was my first day in a new business, with new people and a new environment – why the hell did I want to get stuck behind a computer?

To be completely honest, I didn't like computers and they didn't like me... well, that's what I told myself.

My focus was on people. I wanted to be among my team; that was where I knew I could make a difference. That's where I was going to inspire, influence and make an impact.

Whenever I tell people I didn't have a computer, they always look very confused, so I want to qualify. I didn't have a work computer in my office, but I did have a personal computer in my home office I would take in and out with me daily so that my assistant and the executive teams could email me the necessary, must-see items. I had an amazing assistant to handle the volume of emails for me – why would I want to do her job when she was better at it than me? I would meet with her at the start and end of each day to review emails, and then only the urgent emails would be brought to my attention throughout the day. The rest of the time was dedicated to people and the business.

Think for a moment about how much time you spend on your computer each day responding to emails. Some are necessary; many are *not* necessary.

A Forbes report claims an average office worker receives 200 emails a day, spends 2.5 hours reading and replying to them, and checks their emails 15 times a day. It also claims that the CC and BCC functions waste a lot of time: 144 of the 200 emails received each day are irrelevant.

I didn't want this daily distraction in my life. I wanted to be a visible leader; a leader for the people.

In a study of 21 businesses known for their successful cultures, researchers spent time on site studying the operations and interviewing employees. They found each of the companies, all of which were on 'best places to work' lists, put employees first.

WHY PEOPLE ARE YOUR BIGGEST ASSET

I'm sure you have heard the 'people before profit' concept thrown around at some point in your career. But what does it really mean? For many companies it is wallpaper or window dressing – a recruiting slogan, or a way for them to feel good about themselves.

Research shows that companies that view employees as valuable assets, rather than liabilities, cogs in the wheel or cost centres, outperform companies that don't. This is why it always blows my mind when I hear about companies treating their people like numbers.

Products, marketing campaigns, business strategies, policies, procedures and new initiatives are all created by people; therefore, people should be what matters most to your business. People are your biggest asset!

Just as we go through ups and downs in our personal lives, so do businesses both big and small. Some of these challenges are in our control and others are not. It is important for businesses to stay profitable and continue to invest and grow. This can often lead to changes in direction, process and efficiency reviews, performance analysis and cost cutting, which is all part of running a sustainable and profitable business. It's often the easy stuff, the low-hanging fruit, that goes first: things such as staff incentives, training and coaching and employee perks. All the things that affect morale and the culture of the organisation.

I believe tough times are the most important times to keep morale high and invest in your people.

Having a people-first strategy is what can give you and your organisation a competitive advantage. People who are engaged will do right by the company and when leaders look after their people, the people look after their leaders. They will give their blood, sweat and tears to see their leader's vision advanced. People before profit is not a philosophy; it's an expectation we should all have. You can absolutely put people first and still drive profits.

Putting people at the heart of everything you do builds trust, morale and engagement. This has a very real impact on business success, and has always been part of my leadership style.

Creating a culture of people before profit

⋄ Encourage your people to care for themselves and each other.

⋄ Let people know their work matters, and show them how it affects the bigger picture.

⋄ Be open to ideas and suggestions from people at all levels.

⋄ Create open lines of communication for people to be heard, and value their feedback.

⋄ Invest in your people. Coach, train and develop.

⋄ Treat people like people.

⋄ Put the needs and interests of your people before your own.

⋄ Make the world a better place by giving back.

⋄ Support people through their personal challenges.

BELIEVE IN YOUR PEOPLE

**One of the greatest gifts you can give another human
is to believe in them.**

In chapter 4, I told you the story of my former manager Vivienne, and the impact her words 'I believe in you' had on me at the beginning of my career. The lesson she taught me that day was one that I have taken with me into every role since. I want to be a leader who believes in others and lets them know that I have their back. When people know you believe in them, they do amazing things!

When you believe in someone, it helps them find an inner strength they didn't know they had. It strengthens them emotionally, intellectually and spiritually, and it helps them achieve their potential. Offering simple words of encouragement is among the easiest and most efficient things that we can do to help other people believe in themselves.

CREATE YOUR CHEER SQUAD

Success, happiness and positivity comes from within, but it's also very much about the people we choose to have around us.

When we surround ourselves with positive influences, we feel more energised and motivated. Your cheer squad is the people you can trust to be honest, keep you grounded and listen to you without judgement. You can always count on them to lift your spirits and make you smile.

Who's in your cheer squad?

_____

_____

_____

Life is all about moving forward and it's imperative to be around the right friends, partner, mentors and people who support us, empower us, uplift us and help us live our best life.

My father always told me friendships are about quality not quantity. I remember him saying, 'When I die, if I can count my true friends on one hand, I will be a very lucky man.'

I have taken my father's advice and have surrounded myself with a small group of amazing friends – people who are like-minded, share similar values, would be there for me through thick and thin and lift me up. I hope I do the same for them.

You will come across people who don't want to see you succeed – whether that's because they are jealous, have a lack of ambition or are just 'glass half empty' types. When we surround ourselves with these kinds of negative influences, it drains us of our energy and sense of self. It is important to limit time with or release yourself from these people in your life.

People... are your biggest asset.

People... are your competitive advantage.

People... are the heartbeat of your organisation.

People... follow the leader first, and the vision second.

People... want to belong to something bigger than themselves.

People... are inspired by what you do, not what you say.

People... when given the right environment, will do amazing things.

People... might do what you say, but would they *choose* to follow you?

Nine

THE POWER OF CULTURE

People don't leave bad companies. They leave bad leaders.

BETSY ALLEN-MANNING

$Culture$ can be such a difficult concept to define. It relates to people, purpose and the organisation itself, and how they are all intertwined. However, I think one of the most useful ways to describe culture is this: it is what people do when no-one is watching!

As a leader, one of the areas I have always focused on is creating a culture and an environment that allows people to thrive.

Some might say culture has to do with people from different nationalities, and this is right – to a certain degree. Culture does include race, nationality and ethnicity, but it goes far beyond those identity markers as well.

When I talk about culture, I am referring to a 'way of life'. It encompasses beliefs, values, practices, attitudes and behaviours that people share – not only in the workplace, but also in many areas of our lives, including family life, community, hobbies and even sporting clubs.

From an organisational perspective, culture is the environment that we create for our people. It plays a powerful role in their work satisfaction, retention, relationships, performance and progression.

A great culture is difficult to define but, in general, some of the hallmarks of a strong culture include:

- high staff morale and retention
- ingrained motivation
- a sense of personal responsibility
- an environment of trust and cooperation
- support of creativity and innovation
- investment in people
- clarity of values
- a sense of job security
- open communication
- solid financial performance
- minimal staff politics.

That sounds pretty damn good to me!

So, why do so many organisations struggle to create cultures that engage their people? This is a problem I have always wrestled to understand, because over my 13 years as a CEO my mission was to buck that trend. I wanted to engage, inspire and allow people to bring their best selves to work each day.

As leaders, it is our job to create a culture and environment that allows people to work at their natural best. In turn, organisations grow and thrive.

Culture

noun

Definition: The collective accepted ideas, customs and behaviour of the people within an organisation.

This is part of the reason I adopted a hands-on approach to welcoming new staff to head office. Whenever new team members would join, I would always meet with them to personally welcome them on board, get to know a little about them and share a bit about me and the company direction. This would happen no matter what level of the organisation they were joining.

Once, I went through this process with a new employee, Amber; she was joining the Sportsgirl head office as an assistant to the buying and planning team. Months later, she stopped me as I was walking down the hallway and she said, 'Col, I have to say thank you – I feel so lucky to work here. I feel valued, listened to, supported and, most importantly, I feel safe. I've never felt like this anywhere else I have ever worked. I am so excited to get out of bed in the morning and come to work!'

I recently reached out to Amber to ask her for a few more insights into her experience of the kind and inclusive leadership style I championed at Sportsgirl, and this is what she had to say...

'Each year, we were asked to focus on one simple word: an aspiration or a catalyst for change.

'At our infamous Christmas party, champagne in hand, Col would animatedly recount the year that was and ask each of us to choose our word for the following year.

'The idea was that we would contemplate our word for the year over summer while we travelled, rested and had time to recalibrate. Upon returning to the office, in the haze that is January, we would have had time to reflect on our word as we planned for the year ahead. Some of us kept our word to ourselves, while others shared theirs in the hope of being held accountable. Our words remained ours, never questioned, yet Col encouraged us and gently reminded us to return to our word at all times. That was the thing about Sportsgirl – there was space to be yourself, but there was also space to explore what you could be. The success of the word of the year tradition came from its simplicity, unlike a forgotten new year's resolution.

'I loved witnessing our new starters' joy as they donned their Sportsgirl stripes for the first time during the induction process – each with a sense of wonder as they realised that a tribe like ours could exist in the retail world. In reality, the inspiring and passionate women who made up our brand were the true essence of it. There was always someone cheering you on from the sidelines. Even though we each had chosen unique words to focus on, there was unity and a shared vision among us. It didn't matter when you had joined the tribe or how many birthday celebrations you had been a part of – at the end of the year, you knew, when it came time for Col's much-anticipated Christmas speech, you were as much a part of the dream as every woman standing beside you.'

Amber, new Sportsgirl employee

On that day when Amber stopped me in the corridor, she spoke as if she had just won the career lottery. I thought to myself, *This is how it should be for everyone in every organisation.* It should be a right, not a privilege, for people to feel like this at work.

Of course, creating and nurturing a great culture requires more than just welcoming new members to the team with a personal touch. It's also about how you run the organisation, and the way you empower others to take responsibility for their own careers and achievements.

Later on in this chapter, I'll share some tips and techniques I've used to bolster culture and ensure the environment I'm leading is a place where people can truly shine and achieve their individual goals, with a view to funnelling those achievements into the organisation's overall objectives. But first, let's take a look at why a great culture is so vital.

WHY IS CULTURE IMPORTANT?

Workplace culture affects everything from performance to how an organisation is perceived, both internally and externally. Building a great culture in your organisation will help you entice and retain top talent and improve levels of employee engagement, productivity and performance.

> It doesn't make sense to hire smart people and tell them what to do; we hire smart people so they can tell us what to do.
>
> STEVE JOBS

In my experience, creating a positive culture makes for happier people who are more committed, have greater job satisfaction, perform better and are more likely to stay and grow with the organisation.

Positive culture is something so simple that we all recognise as important, yet it's difficult for many organisations and leaders to implement.

This is why many senior leaders will talk about their competitive advantage as being their strategy, their processes, or even their HR policies. While this might be true to some extent, I believe an organisation's biggest competitive advantage is its people and the culture and environment they work in.

More and more senior-level executives are starting to see the immense value and benefit of cultivating a strong culture. According to a study by *BW Businessworld*, 92 per cent of leaders from successful companies believe that workplace culture has a high impact on a company's financial performance and is critical to reaching financial goals.

Creating a culture of openness, empowerment, collaboration, trust and cooperation is the foundation of a thriving organisation.

A clear, strong, positive and productive culture enables your business to...

⋄ Attract talented staff
⋄ Drive engagement
⋄ Retain the best people
⋄ Improve brand reputation
⋄ Create an environment of growth and development
⋄ Create satisfied employees
⋄ Increase productivity
⋄ Boost financial performance

88 per cent of employees believe a strong company culture is key to business success.

47 per cent of active job-seekers cite culture as their driving reason for looking for a new role.

58 per cent of employees would stay at a lower-paying job if it meant working for a great boss.

79 per cent of employees say they would be more loyal to their employers if they received more recognition.

12 per cent of executives believe their companies are driving the 'right culture'.

66 per cent of job-seekers consider a company's culture and values the most important factor when considering career opportunities.

40 per cent higher employee retention is seen in companies that actively manage their culture.

A GREAT CULTURE STARTS WITH YOU

Creating a great culture is not easy – but it is worth it.

Whether you're a CEO, entrepreneur, senior executive, board member or head of buying, a great culture starts with you. If you are responsible for people, you are also responsible for culture. It starts with you.

> ## Culture is what motivates and retains talented employees.
>
> BETTY THOMPSON

I was once asked by a leader from another organisation, 'Col, when you have half an hour, I would love to pick your brain on how to create a great culture. From everything I've heard, you seem to really be getting this right.'

I was happy to sit down and have a chat but, obviously, creating a strong and supportive culture isn't something you can do in a 30-minute conversation. There is no magic pill for a great culture, and I certainly can't give you the perfect recipe in half an hour. Culture is not something you can buy off the shelf, and nor will a few affirmations or posters around the office do the trick.

Creating a great culture is not about free lunches, free parking or a free pass to the gym, although all of these things are nice to have. These are more like perks – whereas creating a strong culture is something you have to work at every single day.

All of this might make it sound like culture is a lot of work – and, I'm going to be honest, it is. But it's also a very worthwhile investment, because the dividends and pay-off of a positive, productive and empowering workplace culture are immeasurable.

Some leaders might say culture is fluffy and intangible. These leaders are making excuses for not being able to create a great culture.

Culture has to be taught and learned. The kind of culture leaders create in an organisation will determine how employees describe where they work, how connected they feel and how they see themselves as part of the organisation and its future.

My recipe for building a successful culture

- ◇ Give everyone a voice.
- ◇ Recognise individuals are experts in their field.
- ◇ Allow others to take the lead in their own career.
- ◇ Allow feedback and suggestions on big picture thinking.
- ◇ Build an environment founded on trust.
- ◇ Inspire each other.
- ◇ Keep it light and fun.
- ◇ Encourage autonomy throughout the team.
- ◇ Always listen and take other's options onboard.
- ◇ Ensure a high level of engagement with all levels of the team.
- ◇ Never be afraid to jump in and get my hands dirty or help others.
- ◇ Create an environment that allows people to feel part of something bigger than themselves.

FEEDBACK AND RECOGNITION: THE GOLDEN KEYS TO CULTURE

It is human nature to seek validation and want to be recognised. People need to feel that they are valued and that their contributions *matter*.

It perplexes me that so many organisations and leaders find it so hard to give genuine, authentic feedback that lifts their team members up. For me, motivating and encouraging others through recognising their achievements is an 'always on' proposition.

Organisations where recognition occurs have *14 per cent* better employee engagement, productivity and customer service than those without.

Companies with a recognition culture have *31 per cent* lower employee turnover.

75 per cent of employees receiving at least monthly recognition (even if informal) are satisfied with their job.

Peer-to-peer recognition is *35.7 per cent* more likely to have a positive impact on financial results than manager-only recognition.

63 per cent of employees would rather work for a company where people were praised/thanked regularly than for a company that paid 10 per cent more but offered no praise or thanks.

When asked what leaders could do more of to improve engagement, *58 per cent* of respondents replied 'give recognition'.

69 per cent of employees would work harder if they felt their efforts were better appreciated.

50 per cent of employees believe being thanked by managers not only improved their relationship but also built trust with their higher-ups.

When it comes to recognition, it's often the simple things that make the biggest difference. A genuine 'thank you', small words of praise, a handwritten note, little words of encouragement and gestures of appreciation go a long way in reinforcing to people that they are valued. This is the foundation of a positive workplace and the cornerstone of high morale.

There are plenty of tangible things you can do to encourage your staff, such as providing flexible working hours, wellness programs, in-house forums, gym memberships, paid parental leave and employee discounts and rewards. There is nothing wrong with all of these – they sound attractive, fun and, most of all, actionable. As a leader, though, I've found the biggest impact often comes from people being recognised – particularly in front of their peers – whether that be celebrating years-of-service milestones, weekly sales performance, personal achievements, record-breaking successes, or just a job well done.

It's so simple! It's often the smallest things that can have the biggest impact.

THREE QUESTIONS TO ANSWER FOR A POSITIVE CULTURE

To create a culture of trust and cooperation people need to know the answer to three questions:

1. **What is expected of me?**
    People need clear guidelines on what you expect of them.
2. **How is my performance tracking against where I was previously?**
    People want feedback on how they are going
3. **What does my future hold?**
    People need certainty about their future and want to know about any changes that might be in store.

15 WAYS TO CREATE A GREAT CULTURE

There is no easy road to creating a great culture. Each culture is unique to an organisation, just like each of us is unique as an individual. It takes commitment, and consistency, but with the right strategies in place you can encourage a more productive and positive culture to flourish within your workplace.

Here are 15 tips to help you create a great culture:

1. **Encourage relationship-building**

   Strong relationships within the workplace can lead to an increase in effective communication, so look for opportunities for your team members to collaborate and develop deeper relationships. Team-building challenges, group projects and social events are great ways to achieve this.

2. **Provide autonomy**

   Empower people and give them the autonomy to problem solve and make decisions that affect positive change. This will support the growth and development of your team and develop future leaders.

3. **Cultivate open, honest communication**

   Cultivating open and honest communication is a vital ingredient in any organisation. It allows you to create a more engaging, creative and authentic team of people who feel connected to the organisation's goals and vision.

4. **Offer a career path**

   A career path is an essential part of career growth, as well as personal growth and development. A clear pathway ensures people always have a roadmap to follow. A progression pathway is important in retaining great people and, more importantly, creating future leaders. Setting your people up for success means providing the right resources, clear goals and a direction forward.

5. **Create healthy competition**

   Healthy competition can encourage risk-taking and foster resilience and determination. It's a great way to encourage your team to grow. It can also result in increased productivity, motivation and innovation.

6. **Live and breathe your core values**

   Values set the tone for how the organisation behaves. Our core values are what's really important and are the foundation of everything we do and every decision we make. Culture is about living and breathing your core values each and every day.

7. **Focus on collaboration**

   Creating a culture of collaboration allows people to work together, and bring different skills and thinking to the table to achieve a common goal. It also ensures everyone collectively feels valued and appreciated for their contribution.

8. **Promote positivity**

   A positive attitude can lift you up even in hard times. Positivity is contagious and can bring people together, often encouraging accomplishments you never thought possible.

9. **Reward effort**

   Recognition can be one of the greatest motivators. Having their hard work and achievements recognised fuels people to strive for improvement. Let your team members know they are valued; this will inspire them to continuously improve.

10. **Delegate**

    Micromanaging will kill all creativity. If you want your people to achieve above and beyond, you have to let them be free, and be themselves. Of course, you can do this while also setting boundaries and keeping staff accountable. But whenever possible, delegate control. When someone trusts you enough to put you in charge of something, you immediately feel a sense of responsibility and ownership that inspires you to give it your best shot.

11. Share your vision

As a leader, it is crucial to the success of the organisation to share your vision. It provides a sense of purpose and direction and helps with decision-making. How can people know what to do when they don't know where they are going?

12. Push beyond your comfort zone

We stay in our comfort zone because it's just that: comfortable and familiar. It's natural to be scared of failure, but leaving your comfort zone allows you to grow personally and professionally and opens you up to new experiences and opportunities to learn. No-one ever grew by staying in their comfort zone.

13. Encourage life in balance

Life in balance is an important part of a healthy work environment. Maintaining this balance promotes a healthier, happier and more productive workforce, reduces stress and helps prevent burnout.

14. Treat people equally

It goes without saying that you should treat people equally regardless of their position, seniority, race, gender, religion, beliefs, sexual orientation or age. This means giving respect to everyone in your organisation as you strive for equality through an open, honest environment focused on clear communication.

15. Prioritise learning

When we stop learning, we stop growing. Provide both formal and informal ways for your team to learn, upskill and grow. Not only will this increase the skills in your organisation but it will also help your staff feel appreciated for their contributions, which in turn enhances productivity, performance and engagement.

A great culture...

- Demonstrates **strong values**
- Shares a **clear vision** and **purpose**
- Promotes **fairness** and **respect**
- Builds **trust** and **cooperation**
- Fosters a **positive environment**
- Encourages **collaboration**
- Values **everyone's opinions**
- Embraces **individual strengths**
- Celebrates **diversity**
- Creates opportunities to **learn** and **grow**
- Drives **results**
- Is **caring**
- Attracts **great talent**
- Welcomes **new ideas**
- Creates **positive actions**
- Encourages **open** and **honest communication**
- Rewards **teamwork**

CULTURE VERSUS ENVIRONMENT

> You are a product of your environment –
> so choose the environment that will best
> develop you toward your objective.

W CLEMENT STONE

We have all heard the saying that 'people are a product of their environment'. But how does this fit in with culture? Are environment and culture the same thing?

Not quite – but there is a lot of overlap.

I want you to think of yourself as a blank canvas. From the moment you are born, you start painting a picture of yourself on that canvas and this picture is heavily influenced by your surroundings, your experiences and your environments.

We couldn't choose what family we were born into, what suburb we lived in or the type of education we received; all of these decisions were made for us as children. However, these experiences help to shape our beliefs, our values, our likes and dislikes and often what we envisage we want for our future selves.

We may not have had a lot of choice in our environment or circumstances as children, but we can choose how they inform our decisions as adults. We also have control over the type of leader we want to be and the type of leader we want to follow.

Our parents, grandparents or caregivers were responsible for creating loving, nurturing environments that allowed us to grow and shine, influencing our values and beliefs. I credit my parents for many things in life, including the woman and the leader I have become. My mum and dad had very different upbringings, as I mentioned at the start of the book. But there was one thing they both had in common, and that was a belief in the value of hard work.

Just as I was the product of my upbringing, my dad was a product of his. My grandfather was also very hardworking. He migrated from Italy to Australia in the early 1950s, leaving his wife and his two sons behind (one of those being my dad). He arrived in search of a better life.

He travelled on his own, halfway across the world, to a brand new country that was very unfamiliar to him and where he did not speak the language. He arrived with nothing more than hope and optimism on his side, and the focus and discipline to work hard in search of a new beginning for his family.

My parents have always been family-oriented, believing that family comes before anything. This is also my motto, which I translate not only to my own family but also into my working world. I have always seen my work team as an extension of this philosophy – having a close-knit 'work family' is part of what makes work so enjoyable and rewarding for me.

I have always considered my people as someone's daughter or someone's son. I've often asked myself, 'How would I want my children to be treated in the workplace? Would I want them to work in an environment where fear is the motivator, or would I want them to work in an environment where the fear is removed, allowing them to learn, grow and make mistakes? Would I want them to work in an environment filled with animosity and selfishness, or would I want them to work in an environment filled with kindness?'

I have always aimed to create an environment and culture that I would be happy for my own children to work in.

This does not mean I neglected to foster accountability, discipline, honesty and boundaries at work – this is also part of being a great leader.

So consider: does the environment you have created allow people to thrive and shine and do amazing things? How did the environment you grew up in inform the type of leader you are today?

When leaders create an environment where people feel safe, valued, listened to and a part of a team, they set up their people to excel.

When people feel supported, they will raise their hands and say, 'I made a mistake' or 'I need some help' or 'I have a great idea'. When people don't feel supported, the opposite happens. They are scared to make mistakes, they are risk-averse and they become preoccupied with protecting themselves.

People respond to the environment they are in – which is why it is essential, as a strong leader, for you to create an environment that allows others to shine.

> We are all products of our environment;
> every person we meet,
> every new experience or adventure,
> every book we read,
> touches and changes us,
> making us the unique being we are.
>
> CJ HECK

Ask yourself ...

What kind of environment do you want to create? Try to answer in one sentence:

_____

_____

_____

_____

Can you think of examples of other leaders who are doing a very good job with creating a positive and inclusive workplace environment?

_____

_____

_____

_____

_____

_____

_____

_____

What are two to three things you can do to create a more supportive and collaborative environment?

_____

_____

_____

_____

Ten

THE POWER OF
VALUES AND PURPOSE

The Things you are passionate about are not random – They are your calling.

FABIENNE FREDRICKSON

I want to kick this chapter off by asking you a simple question.

Although the question is very straightforward, coming up with an answer can be something else altogether.

That question is...

Who are you?

I'm asking you this question upfront for a specific reason: before you can get started discovering your values and unpacking your purpose, you need to first know yourself.

Now, when you began answering this question, I bet you were coming up with things like:

CEO, artist, entrepreneur, assistant, parent, partner, employee, boss, landlord, client, sister, brother, business owner, student, lawyer, coach, religious leader...

While these are the types of things that represent what you *do*, the hats you wear and the roles you play, they are not an accurate representation of *who you are*.

I want you to ask yourself the question again, but this time, I am putting a rule in place.

*Who are you **without a title**?*

For a moment, I want you to think of yourself as a babushka doll: the outer doll is the face you wear and the personality you present to the world. I want you to dig deeper than this surface-level representation and keep opening the doll, one after the other, until you get right to the core.

It's incredible when I ask this question during my Mentor Me for women programs, because most of the attendees can't answer it. That's okay – I couldn't answer it either when I was first asked.

WHEN I FOUND OUT WHO I WAS

I was fortunate to be given the opportunity to work with a life coach at around the age of 35. Back then, I thought I knew who I was, but I really didn't. I knew what I *did*: I was a career woman, mother, wife, sister, aunty and daughter, but I didn't really know who I was without all of these titles.

I had to put in the hard work to discover who I was:

⬦ What did I believe?

⬦ What was most important to me?

⬦ What wasn't serving me in my life?

⬦ What were my dreams and aspirations?

⬦ What did I want for my future?

After doing some work, I discovered who I am at my core – without all of the titles and roles. I learnt that I am:

- authentic, loving and caring
- a perfectionist
- family oriented
- an all-or-nothing personality
- an achievement junkie
- someone who wants to make a positive impact on other people's lives
- a leader who people choose to follow
- a believer in the power of self
- someone who inspires and empowers people to live their best life
- grateful for what I have, rather than coveting what I don't have.

IT'S TIME TO FIND OUT WHO YOU *REALLY* ARE

When you were younger, did you sometimes find yourself changing your beliefs, behaviours, likes and dislikes and even your personality based on the situation or people you were surrounded by? That's because when we are young we don't really know who we are; we are trying to figure that out, and find our place in the world.

Now you are older (and wiser), so let's find out who you really are. Answer as many or as few of the questions over the next few pages as you like. Don't overthink them. Write down the first things that come to your mind.

And remember:

This is your personal journey of self-discovery.

Asking ourselves questions is one of the most powerful ways to really get in touch with our inner selves and get clarity on the life we want to live.

Only when we truly know ourselves and become comfortable with who we are at the core can we identify and work with our strengths and weaknesses. This is an opportunity to start living our best lives and loving ourselves, because we are being totally honest with the person we see in the mirror.

The following questions might uncover things that you didn't know were weighing you down, bring up some truths about your life that you haven't faced, or help you identify areas you need to work on.

Who am I?

What is most important to me?

_____

_____

_____

What am I most excited about in my life right now?

_____

_____

_____

What am I most grateful for?

_____

_____

_____

If I could change just one thing about my life, what would I change? Why?

_____

_____

_____

What are my greatest strengths?

_____

_____

_____

Who am I?

Who/what inspires me, and why?

_____

_____

_____

What am I afraid of?

_____

_____

_____

What am I putting up with?

_____

_____

_____

How do I want to be remembered by my family?

_____

_____

_____

What does a perfect day look like to me?

_____

_____

_____

Who am I?

If I had six months left to live, what would I change?

_____

_____

_____

What's holding me back from living the life I want to live?

_____

_____

_____

What puts a smile on my face no matter what?

_____

_____

_____

Have I ever felt truly loved by myself or someone else?

_____

_____

_____

Do I ever have self-doubt? Why?

_____

_____

_____

Who am I?

What is my happiest memory?

_____

_____

_____

If I could have any career, what would it be?

_____

_____

_____

What am I truly passionate about?

_____

_____

_____

What gifts or talents do I have but don't share with others?

_____

_____

_____

When I have free time, what do I like to do for fun?

_____

_____

_____

Who am I?

What do I hope my legacy will be?

_____

_____

_____

Which aspects of my life do I worry about?

_____

_____

_____

What is my proudest accomplishment in life?

_____

_____

_____

How would others describe me?

_____

_____

_____

What would I consider to be my biggest failure in life?

_____

_____

_____

Who am I?

What has been my biggest life lesson?

_____

_____

_____

Are there areas of my life where I compare myself to others? Why?

_____

_____

_____

What are my goals – short-term and long-term?

_____

_____

_____

What do I believe is possible in my life?

_____

_____

_____

What do I really want for my future?

_____

_____

_____

WHAT ARE VALUES, AND WHY DO WE NEED THEM?

Values are what is most important in your life – those things that really matter to you; the ideas and beliefs that you deem to be most significant in the way you live and work.

As I said in chapter 4, your values have likely been influenced by a range of things, including your background, events that have happened or you have witnessed, your upbringing or maybe your spiritual beliefs.

You've probably learned many of your values from your parents, your grandparents, your teachers, your religious leaders, your coach and the people around you.

Your values are an important part of who you are – and who you want to be. They highlight what you want to stand for, and represent your uniqueness. In my experience, knowing our values allows us to have greater fulfilment in the way we live our lives.

The most important thing about knowing your values is that they give you clarity with your decision-making.

> **Values guide your behaviours and
> provide you with an inner compass and
> personal code of conduct to live by.**

When you make decisions in line with your values, you will have a strong sense of integrity, clarity and confidence. You will feel more content and in control of your life. Have you ever made a decision and found that it just didn't feel right – it didn't sit comfortably? (Some call it a gut feeling.) That's because your decision wasn't aligned with your values. In my experience, if it feels wrong it probably *is* wrong.

So, consider:

- How would you define your values?
- What is most important in your life?

- What must you have in your life to experience fulfilment?
- What values are essential to supporting your inner self?
- Is a higher salary more important than your sanity?
- Does career come before your health and wellbeing?
- Are you prioritising others before yourself?
- Have you ever made a decision that felt wrong, but you followed through with it anyway? What was the outcome?

This chapter will help you find clarity around some of these questions.

When I first started writing the Mentor Me for women program, I began writing about leadership, because that's what I'm really passionate about. But as I started writing, I realised that we need to be leading in our own lives before we can be leading anyone else. This means knowing ourselves, our values and our purpose.

These are our foundations. I liken it to building a house: if you don't build strong foundations first, it is not going to be standing for too long. Cracks will start to appear, and it won't weather the external factors such as storms and strong winds. We as humans are exactly the same.

If we don't build solid foundations for ourselves, we won't be able to weather the challenges that life throws at us.

Most people when asked can't articulate what's most important to them. Often, we assume our values are those that our society, culture and the external world values – but if we dig deeper to discover our own values, we may find they are quite different.

It's only once you start to do this work that you can discover what you truly value, at a personal level. It may be (and is likely to be) different from what your friend, sister or neighbour values most. This is where knowing your values can be so powerful – because if you're not clear on your own values, you can end up living your life according to someone else's.

Values have been a big part of my experience and approach as a leader. An awareness of values has set the tone for not only how I have behaved as a leader and what's important to me, but also how my leadership extends through an organisation.

I am extremely perplexed and concerned when I speak to leaders and organisations and they don't even know their values. Leaders are responsible for setting the tone for how the organisation behaves. If they aren't clear on their values, how on earth can their teams be clear?

HOW TO IDENTIFY YOUR VALUES

There are many different ways you can identify your values and arrive at a shortlist, although it can seem to be a daunting task at first.

I'm often asked what the ideal number of values is. If you have too few, you can find yourself focusing on a range that is far too narrow to have any real impact when it comes to guiding your decisions and choices in life. If you have too many, you'll forget them, be overwhelmed, or won't be focused, and it then becomes hard to truly live by them.

While the number of values differs for each person, in my experience and for the purpose of this exercise I suggest landing on five values. So, I'm going to keep it nice and simple for you with five easy steps to finding your values that will serve you in every area of your life and work.

Ready? Take out your pen and let's get started.

Step 1: Identify

Circle 12 to 15 values that speak to you from the list below. Don't think too hard about them — just choose the ones that resonate most.

Achievement	Environment	Learning
Advancement	Equality	Legacy
Adventure	Fairness	Love
Affection	Faith	Loyalty
Authenticity	Fame	Nature
Authority	Family	Openness
Autonomy	Financial security	Optimism
Balance	Forgiveness	Order
Beauty	Freedom	Peace
Boldness	Friendship	Personal development
Career	Fun	Pleasure
Challenge	Generosity	Popularity
Change	Gratitude	Power
Comfort	Growth	Recognition
Communication	Happiness	Relationships
Community	Health	Religion
Compassion	Honesty	Reputation
Competition	Humanity	Respect
Contribution	Humour	Responsibility
Cooperation	Influence	Self-respect
Cooperative	Inner harmony	Spirituality
Creativity	Inspiration	Stability
Culture	Integrity	Status
Curiosity	Involvement	Success
Determination	Justice	Teamwork
Discipline	Kindness	Trust
Empathy	Knowledge	Wealth
Energy	Leadership	Wisdom

Define your priorities,
know your values and
believe in your purpose.
Only then can you
effectively share yourself
with others.

LES BROWN

Step 2: Prioritise

Rank your chosen values in order of importance from 1 to 12, with 1 being the most important. This is often the most challenging part because you might already be cutting out three from the list!

1. _____

2. _____

3. _____

4. _____

5. _____

6. _____

7. _____

8. _____

9. _____

10. _____

11. _____

12. _____

Step 3: Express

Next, take the top five values from your list and write next to each of them what they *really* mean to you. (Leave the third column in the table blank for now.)

	Value	What does this value mean to you?	What do you need to add, delete or change to reflect this value?
1.			
2.			
3.			
4.			
5.			

Step 4: Reflect

Once you've completed your list of values, walk away from them and revisit them again the next day. Review your list and consider:

- How do they make you feel?

_____

_____

- Do you feel they are consistent with who you are? Why are they personal to you?

_____

_____

- Do you see any values that feel inconsistent with your identity and not reflective of the real you?

_____

_____

- Check your priority ranking. Do you feel like your values are in the proper order of importance?

_____

_____

Do the five values you have chosen feel right?

If so, put them somewhere you can see them daily. Write them on the whiteboard in your office, have them as a screensaver or put them on your phone.

If they don't feel quite right, go back and revisit step 1 and choose values from the original list again, and complete the next steps again until you are happy with your selection.

Step 5: Pledge

Now that you are happy with your values, it's time to work out what you need to change, add or delete in your life to reflect and start optimally living these values. Go back and note this in your list.

You might not be living your values right now, but you have taken the first step to identifying them and you soon will be. Once you have identified your values, they will act as your inner compass for all of your decision-making from here on in.

Also remember that your values may change as you move through life. For example, when you start your career, you might measure success by money and status and this might be your priority at this stage in your life. But after you have a family, a life in balance may be what you value more. You might like to come back to this exercise at different times in your life to see how your values change.

Keep this book handy and jot down your changed values here:

_____

_____

_____

_____

_____

_____

_____

_____

_____

_____

Every day, work harder on yourself than anything else. If you become more intelligent, more valuable, more skilled, you will add more value to others.

TONY ROBBINS

ARE YOU LIVING YOUR PERSONAL VALUES?

Now that you have chosen your top five values, let's see how well you're living them. Here are some examples to get you thinking about how you may or may not be living in alignment with your values.

Family

If your value is **family** but you:

- are working 60 hours a week
- are always too tired to spend intimate or quality time with your partner
- often find yourself on a screen so you can multitask while watching your kids
- never switch off and enjoy time with your family...

... it's time to change, add or delete something.

Health

If your value is **health** but you:

- don't eat well
- don't get enough sleep
- don't find enough time to exercise because you're 'too busy'
- don't value your quality of life...

... it's time to change, add or delete something.

Achievement

If your value is **achievement** but you:

- find it hard to get started on new things
- don't put yourself forward for promotions or awards

- tend to start 10 projects but never manage to finish one
- don't set goals, but just hope for the best...

... it's time to change, add or delete something.

Wealth

If your value is **wealth** but you:
- don't have any savings or a savings plan
- don't respect money by staying up-to-date on your bills and budget
- spend more than you earn
- waste money on things that don't genuinely add value to your life...

... it's time to change, add or delete something.

Self-respect

If your value is **self-respect** but you:
- constantly talk down to yourself
- have persistent negative thoughts
- don't stand up for yourself at work or at home
- allow others to treat you poorly
- question whether you are 'good enough'...

... then it's time to change, add or delete something.

Remember, nothing changes if nothing changes!

My example: Kindness, integrity, achievement, family, health.

The big questions

When you know your values, you can use them to make decisions about how to live your life. Your values can help you answer questions like:

⬦ What job or career should I pursue?

⬦ Should I accept this promotion/opportunity/ job?

⬦ Should I start my own business?

⬦ Is this relationship good for me?

⬦ Should I compromise, or be firm with my position?

⬦ Should I follow tradition, or travel down a new path?

⬦ Is this a risk worth taking?

⬦ Am I on track to create the kind of life I want for myself?

⬦ Does my current lifestyle genuinely bring me joy?

⬦ Why am I not achieving the goals I have set myself?

MY VALUES STORY

As part of my toolkit for recovery from burnout, I was fortunate to work with a life coach: the incredible Shannah Kennedy. At our first session, she asked me two questions:

1. Who are you?

2. What are your values?

I had no idea how to answer either question.

I didn't know who I was without my job and I certainly hadn't identified my values – which is why and how I had ended up in this place of burnout.

It was clear I had a lot of work to do... on myself!

I soon identified that one of my values was health, and many things needed to change for me to start living that value. I committed to cultivating a lifelong focus on my health and wellbeing.

Clarifying this value as a top priority highlighted many things I needed to change, add and delete in my life. I needed to build in self-care, set boundaries, share the load and learn to say 'no' more often. Identifying and pledging my values allowed me to build habits into my life that would better serve me (and those around me).

Even today, many years later, health is still at the top of my priority list and is an essential aspect of the way I live my life.

**Living by your values is even more important
than focusing on your goals:
you might not always reach your goals,
but you can always choose to live by your values.**

THE POWER OF PURPOSE

If you want to be happy and content, and experience inner peace and ultimate fulfilment, it's critical that you learn how to find your passion and life purpose.

Your life purpose is the reason you get up in the morning and what puts a fire in your belly. It is why you show up; the message you wish to share with the world.

Like your values, your purpose can also guide your life decisions, shape your goals, give you a sense of direction and create meaning in your life.

**Knowing your purpose helps you
live life with integrity – you know who you are,
what you are and why you are.**

When you know yourself, it becomes easier to live a fulfilled life that's in line with your values.

You might see your life purpose described as your life direction, purpose statement, life mission or 'why'. The words might be different, but all of these mean the same thing.

If you are not clear on your purpose, you might find yourself heading down the wrong path. Your goals may not be aligned to your purpose; you might find yourself continually pursuing goals, only to realise when you achieve them that you don't feel any more fulfilled.

On the other hand, when you know your purpose, that's when conscious living begins. That's when you feel excited and alive. It doesn't mean that life is smooth sailing, but at least you know what you want to do and be in this world. With a clear purpose, you can set the right goals and plans, and take the right steps to create your most meaningful life.

Brand purpose

Before we move on to fully explore your personal life purpose, I want to take a moment to talk about brand purpose.

> **Brand purpose is essentially a brand's reason for being, beyond making money. Brands that have a strong purpose connect with their consumers on a much deeper emotional level.**

I want you to think for a moment of a brand that you believe has a strong purpose – a strong belief or reason for being that goes beyond what it sells.

A brand that has a strong purpose:

- adds value not just to the lives of customers but also to society as a whole
- builds emotional relationships with its customers
- is differentiated from its competitors through its purpose
- builds a connection beyond what it sells.

On the next pages, I'm going to share a few of my favourite brand purposes with you.

These are powerful examples of brands that have a strong purpose, a soul and the ability to connect with customers on a much more meaningful and deeper level.

I believe the brands that do this will thrive in the future and make a positive impact on the world.

'Our purpose is to unite the world through sport
to create a healthy planet, active communities and
an equal playing field or all.'

Nike

'Beauty should be a source of confidence, and not
anxiety. That's why we are here to help women
everywhere develop a positive relationship with the
way they look, helping them raise their self-esteem
and realise their full potential.'

Dove

'Our purpose is to help parents and educators raise
creatively-alive kids. We want to help kids ask those
"what if?" questions that keep them curious.
So, our goal is to free the "what if?" questions
in kids' minds.'

Crayola

'The Body Shop exists to fight for a fairer, more
beautiful world. Our business is a force for good,
the empowerment of women and girls and
the belief that everyone is beautiful.'

The Body Shop

'To accelerate the world's transition to
sustainable energy.'

Tesla

'We appreciate that all life on earth is under threat
of extinction. We aim to use the resources we have
– our business, our investments, our voice and our
imaginations – to do something about it.'

Patagonia

'To create a better everyday life for the many people.'

IKEA

If you can't figure out your purpose, figure out your passion. For your passion will lead you right into your purpose.

BISHOP TD JAKES

Personal purpose

Each of us is born with a unique life purpose. For some people, their purpose and passion in life is obvious and clear, but for others it's not. One thing I believe to be true is that we are born with talents and skills that we develop over time.

Think of yourself as a child. What were the things that you were naturally good at? If I take my children, for example, it was clear very early in childhood what they were interested in.

Jake, who is now in his 20s, loved to read and learn. He was good at school, focused, diligent and always asked questions. It was easy to see from an early age that he was going to be the academic one. Jake lived in Japan for a year and attended university in Kyoto (he now speaks fluent Japanese), and is now in the final stages of completing a double degree majoring in International Business and Japanese at Monash University.

Trent, who is also now in his 20s, always enjoyed being the centre of attention. He was the class clown and the entertainer at every party. He loved to make people laugh. He is a total people connector and everyone who meets him has an instant attraction to his incredible spirit and zest for life. Trent recently completed a course at the National Institute of Dramatic Art (NIDA), Australia's leading centre for education and training in the performing arts, and is now pursuing his acting career.

The youngest of the clan, Macey, is a teenager. From as early as I can remember, Macey loved raiding my wardrobe and dressing up. She loved high heels, dresses, jewellery and make-up, which always ended in a lounge room concert or catwalk performance. She always loved singing, dancing and entertaining, and still does. Macey is incredibly talented: she sings, writes songs and is a self-taught guitarist.

All my kids had natural talents that were clear indicators of what they would end up ultimately being passionate about and wish to pursue in life.

For some people, though, it's not as easy to identify their passion. You may have even asked yourself at one point or another:

'What should I do with my life?'

'What is my passion?'

'What is my life's purpose?'

Alternatively, you may enjoy what you do in your career, but when you dig deeper you may discover that you're passionate about something completely different.

When you know your purpose, you start living a little more fully every day. Are you ready to uncover yours? Remember: your purpose is not something you need to make up, it's already there – waiting to be discovered.

Keep your thoughts positive because your thoughts become **your words**.

Keep your words positive because your words become **your behaviour**.

Keep your behaviour positive because your behaviour becomes **your habits**.

Keep your habits positive because your habits become **your values**.

Keep your values positive because your values become **your destiny**.

MAHATMA GANDHI

My purpose...

What do I love to do?

My example: Painting, being adventurous, connecting with nature, camping, cooking, entertaining, helping others, leading others, mentoring, travelling, trying new things, playing music, parenting, storytelling, gardening, coding, writing, studying...

_____

_____

_____

_____

_____

What comes easily to me?

My example: Adapting, positivity, believing in others, inspiring, encouraging, learning, memorising, optimism, listening, problem-solving, kindness, risk-taking, sharing, resilience...

_____

_____

_____

_____

_____

What are two qualities I most enjoy expressing in the world?

My example: Kindness and authenticity.

_____

_____

My purpose...

How do I express these qualities?

My example: I express mine by inspiring and empowering people.

_____

_____

_____

What would a perfect world look like to you?

My example: My perfect world is a world where people get up every day feeling inspired, lead with kindness, love what they do and have the confidence to lead in their own lives, sharing the best version of themselves with the world.

_____

_____

_____

_____

Now that you've gone through this process, you can create your purpose statement.

My example: To be an authentic human who makes a positive impact in people's lives. To inspire and empower others to feel confident, lead in their own lives, show kindness and be the best version of themselves.

_____

_____

_____

_____

_____

Purpose statements to inspire you

'*My purpose* is to stand up for issues that I believe in and contribute positively to my community. I want to leave this world better than I found it.'

'*My purpose* is to find success in my career. I want to be someone of great integrity and be valued for my contributions.'

'*My purpose* is to be a caretaker of the earth and to prevent or reduce harmful effects of human activities on our ecosystem.'

'*My purpose* is to raise a family of caring, loving, passionate and independent children who are fulfilled, find success and live with integrity.'

'*My purpose* is to live a life in service of others. I want to be fulfilled in my work and find meaning through philanthropy. I want to die knowing I made an impact on those around me.'

'*My purpose* is to be an educator and help students reach their greatest potential. I want to help young kids find happiness and success through learning.'

'*My purpose* is to live my life in balance. I want to achieve harmony between my career, my family and fun.'

'*My purpose* is to be my true self, uninhibited by fear. I want to inspire others to live with authenticity and radiate positivity.'

HOW PURPOSE MOVES YOU FORWARD

Personally, my purpose has evolved over the years – just as I have. That said, I always knew I wanted to help people. I wanted to inspire and empower others through my leadership, and my own story and experiences.

My purpose today is stronger than ever, and I know that this is what I was put on the earth to do.

I work with so many women every day of all ages who are just now finding their purpose. I want to inspire them to live with confidence, have a voice, lead in their own lives, change the rules, embrace their superpowers and live a life filled with purpose.

> **When you are clear on your purpose,**
> **you can stop wasting time pursuing the**
> **things you thought you wanted and needed,**
> **and start living a life of meaning and fulfilment.**
> **You can focus your energy on the**
> **things that are really important.**

Instead of wasting your time in a job you don't love, you can work towards a career that inspires and empowers you, and aligns with your purpose.

Instead of living a life without true meaning, you can create a life of meaning and fulfilment.

Instead of being in a toxic relationship, you can find the person who shares the same values as you.

Instead of just going through the motions, you can create a life full of passion and purpose while achieving your goals.

When we know our purpose,
we move from...

what we do

to

why we do it.

Your work doesn't end just because you have found your purpose: you still need to put in the hard work to make things happen. But once you have found your purpose, you'll know the right road to travel down.

When you know your life purpose, you will be filled with energy and passion and be excited to start each day. You will be inspired by what is possible and what you can create.

Your life has purpose.

Your story is important.

Your dreams count.

Your kindness is contagious.

Your voice matters.

Your spark ignites others.

Your life is your creation.

A FINAL WORD

As you come to the end of this book, I have one hope for you:

**I hope your cup is full, your soul is singing,
you are bursting with confidence and
you feel armed with the strategies and tools
you need to live your best life!**

I want to thank you for taking the time to read *Leader by Design* and, more importantly, I want to thank you for investing in the most important person: you. I hope this book has:

- helped you reconnect with yourself
- given you some actionable insights on leadership
- helped you to find your own unique superpowers
- inspired you to change, add or delete the things that aren't quite working in your life, so you can live with purpose and fulfilment.

Nothing gives me more joy and happiness than living my purpose to inspire and empower those around me to lead with confidence in their own lives. Whether you're a mum, leader, carer, artist, coach or entrepreneur (or a mix of any of these!) I hope I have done that for you.

OUR LIVES ARE LIKE A BOOK

At the beginning of 2020, I started writing both this book and a new chapter of my life: one that I want to share with the world; one where my purpose plays out deeply and broadly each and every day.

What I have realised while writing the book is that our lives are just like a book. As we turn each page and complete each chapter, we are writing our own unique stories – in our careers, relationships, businesses and everyday lives.

Many people might identify the start of a new chapter as a major life event, such as getting married, starting a business, launching a new career or moving to a new city – but the truth is, you can start a new chapter whenever you want to.

Each new day is a new page and each new chapter is an opportunity to add to your story.

No-one else is writing your story – it's up to you. Until you write the final sentence, you have time to change the story. Remember: change your story and you can change your life!

When you write that last sentence, what do you want it to say? What story do you want to tell?

Will your book be full of unforgettable moments, stories of a life lived with purpose, tales of inspiration and the positive impact you had on others; or will it be full of 'what ifs', 'I should haves' and 'I could haves'?

Will it be a love story, a comedy, a story of self-discovery, one of lifetime adventures full of achievements, or one of incredible resilience?

Yesterday is the past, today is the present and tomorrow is the future – and you have the opportunity to reimagine that future story. We can't rewrite the past but we can live in the present moment and shape the future that we want for ourselves and those around us.

Let's not look back on our lives and have regrets. *Why did I stay in that relationship, why didn't I put my hand up for that promotion, why didn't I follow my heart, why did I say no, why did I lose contact with that friend, why didn't I change careers sooner...*

Sitting in these types of thoughts can leave us stuck. No matter where you are in your life right now, right at this moment, consider: tomorrow is a new day. Tomorrow you get the opportunity to start writing that new chapter in your life.

Don't look back – you're not going that way.

MARY ENGELBREIT

I want to leave you with a couple of final thoughts that I wish someone had shared with my younger self.

THERE IS NO SUCH THING AS PERFECT

For me, perfectionism started at a very young age. Often, perfectionists grow up with unrealistic expectations from their parents, grandparents or carers, or are perhaps competing with a sibling, but for me perfectionism started with *me*.

It was the pressure I put on myself, because I desperately wanted my parents to be proud of me. In the early days while I was building my career, striving for perfection served me well because it made me push myself as hard as I could go, always aiming to be better, with a high benchmark for personal excellence and a 'never give up' attitude.

But in my adult years, particularly when I had children, it only led to disappointment and exhaustion. I was trying to be the perfect mother, wife, boss, friend and sister. It was an impossible benchmark. Perfection doesn't exist, it just sets us up for failure. Once I acknowledged this (or maybe I just learnt the hard way), I moved from 'striving for perfection' to 'just doing my best', and it freed my mind to appreciate what I have and cut myself some slack.

So I want to encourage you to move from that place of striving for perfection (an ideal that just doesn't exist) to telling yourself every day: 'I'm doing my best, and my best is always good enough'.

FIND MOMENTS TO CELEBRATE - EVERY DAY, IN EVERY WAY

Especially in this modern, fast-paced world we live in, where we are constantly connected and comparing ourselves on social media, it's important to find the 'wins' in everyday life and to celebrate them.

When I reframed my thinking and changed the story I was telling myself, I also decided to adopt a mindset of gratitude that includes noticing the things I do well, celebrating the wins (big and small) and telling myself that I am good enough, and that 'my best' is good enough, too.

I want you to tell yourself the following every day (and, more importantly, I want you to believe it!):

- I'm doing my best.
- I love and accept myself.
- I am enough.
- I don't need other people's approval.
- I am worthy.
- I am beautiful.

The best time to repeat these phrases is when you notice yourself in the midst of focusing on what you 'lack'. Instead of focusing on your perceived flaws, find a way to celebrate the things you are grateful for. It's a total game changer.

BELIEVE IN YOURSELF

Finally, the last thing I want to leave you with is the importance of believing in yourself.

Self-belief is the beginning of your journey and will open up endless possibilities – but it starts with you. There are many factors in life that will contribute to your success but the biggest will be your self-belief.

Believing in yourself means having faith in your own abilities, trusting that you can do anything you put your mind to. It means that when you face challenges, hit road bumps or fall over and have self-doubt, you will have the confidence to get back up and try again. It is not opportunities, intelligence or resources that allow you to chase your goals and dreams – it's your belief in yourself that will give you the power to take that first step.

So, start believing. Apply for that promotion, write that song, sign up to that course, start that new business, ask him or her on that first date, write that book.

You are amazing, talented, beautiful and unique and there is only ever going to be one of you, so believe in yourself.

Start right now. Start believing in *you!*

⁓

Nothing I have written in this book is easy... but I promise you it's worth it.

It's time to step up, have a voice and be the game changer for your generation and future generations.

It's time for us all to lead with kindness, empathy and compassion.

It's time to believe in yourself and your ability, embrace your superpower, share your voice, step up and take action. I want you to believe in the power of self and that it is possible to become the leader you always wanted to be, in business and in life. It's the responsibility of us all to create a kinder world and a new era of leadership.

I want to see women supporting women, so that we can all flourish in all areas of our lives – not just in our careers. Lifting each other up, being great role models, building real confidence and encouraging each other to reach our full potential is the only way we can make change. Remember: we all have the ability to be leaders in our own lives, and you don't need a title to do that.

Often the only thing that is holding us back is ourselves. So follow your dreams, write your story, live with purpose and shine bright, wherever this journey called life takes you. Your new chapter starts now!

ABOUT THE AUTHOR

Colleen Callander, former Sportsgirl CEO and founder of Mentor Me

Geelong born and raised, Colleen was brought up in a hardworking business-focused family where there was always a job to do. After working in family businesses from as young as she could remember, Colleen had her first taste of retail at the age of 16. Unbeknown to her at the time, this summer job would be the start of a retail career spanning over 30 years.

Colleen is an award-winning CEO with a proven track record in building brands, creating winning cultures and building environments that allow people to be inspired and empowered.

Colleen is an inspiration to women of all generations. She wants to encourage women to have the confidence to believe in themselves and their abilities, share their voices and find their inner superpowers. With this book, she aims to inspire and empower women to lead in their own lives – whether that be in boardrooms, organisations, communities or even the home. She wants women to believe it is possible to become the leader they always wanted to be, in business and in life. Together, women can create a new era of leadership – one that is centred in kindness, humility and self-awareness, and that puts people at its heart.

Colleen is a **leader by design**. In the early years of her career, she looked up to and admired people with titles, levels of authority and positions of power, labelling them leaders. She learnt over time that it isn't someone's title that qualifies them for leadership. In fact, Colleen shares that you don't even need a title to be a leader. We all have the ability to lead every day, with every action, every reaction, every interaction and every decision.

BEYOND THE BOOK

In this book, Colleen shares her story of finishing school at 16 and building her career from the ground up, becoming one of Australia's inspiring female CEOs. Her story underpins her message that anything is possible in business and in life if you are passionate, work hard and believe in yourself.

Speaking

Colleen is a sought-after keynote speaker, guest panellist and thought leader. Her keynotes are highly engaging and inspire the audience to step up, have a voice, live with purpose, own their superpower and have self-belief. She shares simple tools and actionable plans to empower participants to navigate through challenges and lead in their own lives. She shares her thoughts on life in balance, her comeback from burnout and the power of building confidence.

Mentoring

As a former CEO of two of Australia's iconic fashion brands, Colleen is proud to be a female leader who has led with purpose, stayed true to her values, inspired and empowered women to believe in themselves and created a culture that allowed people to truly shine. She now believes that it is time to share her purpose and passion with all women, which is the reason she launched Mentor Me.

Mentor Me is the platform through which Colleen mentors women from different walks of life. Executives, mums, start-up entrepreneurs, young women starting out in their careers, travel consultants, senior leaders, teachers... Colleen has worked with all of these women and more!

One-on-one mentoring is tailored to your individual needs, while group mentoring is run in small groups as a four-week program.

Colleen will challenge you to step outside your comfort zone and set boundaries and goals that empower you to take action.

Leadership and business coaching

Working with Colleen is a once-in-a-lifetime opportunity to give your business a competitive edge. With 30 years' experience in retail and 13 years as CEO, Colleen is an incredible asset to any business. Colleen will guide and support your business through change management, strategic direction and brand differentiation, or help you build a culture of success empowerment.

Contact Colleen today for more information, booking enquiries and bulk book sales enquiries.

Email: colcallander@gmail.com
Web: www.colleencallander.com.au
Instagram: instagram.com/colleen_callander

WHAT PEOPLE SAY ABOUT MENTOR ME

'I took the chance to invest in myself, not really sure what to expect. As a result of Colleen's mentoring I emerged, just weeks later, a self-assured woman and leader. Colleen is honest, passionate and understanding and will encourage you to step out of your comfort zone. Sharing the experience with other like-minded women means that you're never alone in the journey of self-discovery.'

Rebecca

'I have found the Mentor Me program to be highly valuable and inspiring. I would recommend this program to any female leaders looking to empower themselves and connect with like-minded leaders.'

Nadia

'The Mentor Me program is a fantastic way to connect with an inspirational, diverse group of women and learn from Colleen Callander, a truly incredible leader and role model.'

Briony

'The Mentor Me program was exactly what I needed in my life. After each session I felt empowered, motivated and inspired. The exercises really peeled back some layers and made me aware of who I am, and that my purpose is more than just being a mum. It was so nice to share each others' experiences and hear about Col's journey throughout her working and personal life. There are so many things I will take from the program to use in all aspects of my life.'

Hayley

'Deciding to spend money on myself right now was not easy, but it's been the best investment in self-reflection and personal development. Inspiring, practical and thought provoking – it's been a special and safe gift from Colleen and my fellow Mentor Me participants.'

Lisa

'I highly recommend working with Colleen and the Mentor Me program to anyone looking to take a deep dive into exploring their values, purpose and leadership. Colleen's take on leadership is a breath of fresh air and meeting with like-minded women in a small group format adds to the experience.'

Amy

ACKNOWLEDGEMENTS

I want to thank my husband, Nick, for his endless love and unwavering belief in me and for making me laugh every day. Thank you for always having my back and being by my side on this crazy journey called life!

Jake, Trent and Macey: you all inspire me every day to be a better mum and human. I love watching you all grow and write your own stories and I learn from you each and every day. I couldn't be more proud of you all... I love you to the moon and back!

My mum and dad, who I credit for the woman and leader I am today: I am so extremely grateful that I got the best of both of you in my genes and habits. You give me unconditional love and support and I love you both with all of my heart.

To my siblings, Richard and Lisa: we have a unique bond that can never be broken. Thank you for enriching my life with seven beautiful nieces and a nephew, and for your love and support. Lisa, you are not only my sister but also my best friend and I love you.

To my cheer squad (you all know who you are): thank you for your encouragement, support and belief in me to write this book. And, of course, thank you to all of my wonderful friends who make life's journey so much fun.

Thank you to my teams – every single one of you past and present who have inspired me to get up every day, stay true to my values, live with purpose and be a better leader.

Thank you to everyone who helped me write this book, from editors and publishers, to those who gave me an encouraging pep talk or connected me with others who could help bring this from an idea to reality.

Lastly, to all the women in the Mentor Me community: you inspire me with your stories each and every day. There is a little bit of each of you in this book. Keep shining and remember that the best is yet to come.

REFERENCES

Chapter 1

Wigert, Ben & Agrawal, Sangeeta (2018), 'Employee Burnout, Part 1: The 5 Main Causes', Gallup, gallup.com/workplace/237059/employee-burnout-part-main-causes.aspx.

Stahl, Ashley (2016), 'Here's What Burnout Costs You', *Forbes*, forbes.com/sites/ashleystahl/2016/03/04/heres-what-burnout-costs-you/?sh=56af056b4e05.

Borysenko, Karlyn (2019), 'Burnout Is Now An Officially Diagnosable Condition: Here's What You Need To Know About It', *Forbes*, forbes.com/sites/karlynborysenko/2019/05/29/burnout-is-now-an-officially-diagnosable-condition-heres-what-you-need-to-know-about-it/?sh=7b6c6ad92b99.

Australian Government Workplace Gender Equality Agency (2020), 'Australia's gender equality scorecard', wgea.gov.au/data/wgea-research/australias-gender-equality-scorecard.

Royal, Ken (2019), 'What Engaged Employees Do Differently', Gallup, gallup.com/workplace/266822/engaged-employees-differently.aspx.

Chapter 4

Zenger, Jack (2018), 'The Confidence Gap In Men And Women: Why It Matters And How To Overcome It', *Forbes*, forbes.com/sites/jackzenger/2018/04/08/the-confidence-gap-in-men-and-women-why-it-matters-and-how-to-overcome-it/?sh=3dca853f3bfa.

KPMG (2015), 'KPMG Women's Leadership Study: Moving Women Forward into Leadership Roles', assets.kpmg/content/dam/kpmg/ph/pdf/ThoughtLeadershipPublications/KPMGWomens LeadershipStudy.pdf.

Lipman, Joanne (2018), 'Women are still not asking for pay rises. Here's why', World Economic Forum, weforum.org/agenda/2018/04/women-are-still-not-asking-for-pay-rises-here-s-why/.

Cover Media (2020), 'New study reveals just how many thoughts we have each day', Newshub, newshub.co.nz/home/lifestyle/2020/07/new-study-reveals-just-how-many-thoughts-we-have-each-day.html.

Chapter 6

William Baker & Michael O'Malley (2008), *Leading with Kindness: How Good People Consistently Get Superior Results*, HarperCollins Focus.

Oswald, Andrew J, Proto, Eugenio & Sgroi, Daniel (2009), 'Happiness and productivity', *Journal of Labor Economics*, December.

Chapter 8

Acton, Annabel (2017), 'How To Stop Wasting 2.5 Hours On Email Every Day', *Forbes*, 13 July, forbes.com/sites/annabelacton/2017/07/13/innovators-challenge-how-to-stop-wasting-time-on-emails/?sh=6260c19e9788.

Britt, Rober Roy (2020), 'Beyond the Bottom Line: Why Putting People First Matters', US Chamber of Commerce, 17 August, uschamber.com/co/start/strategy/putting-employees-before-profits.

Chapter 9

BW Online Bureau (2017), '92% Leaders Believe That "Workplace Culture Has A High Impact On A Company's Financial Performance"', *BW Businessworld*, bwpeople.businessworld.in/article/92-Leaders-Believe-That-Workplace-Culture-Has-A-High-Impact-On-A-Company-s-Financial-Performance-/12-09-2017-125940/.

Heinz, Kate (2019), '42 shocking company culture statistics you need to know', Built In, builtin.com/company-culture/company-culture-statistics.

Previte, Jeff (2020), 'The Best Company Culture Statistics in 2020 to Help You Improve Productivity', Business 2 Community, business2community.com/workplace-culture/the-best-company-culture-statistics-in-2020-to-help-you-improve-productivity-02337682.

Dabash, Hend (n.d.), '21 employee recognition statistics worth memorising', RewardGateway, rewardgateway.com/au/blog/21-key-employee-recognition-statistics.

Son, Sabrina (2016), '12 Mind-Blowing Stats on Employee Recognition You Need to Know', Tinypulse, tinypulse.com/blog/sk-employee-recognition-stats.

We would love you to follow Colleen on:

- instagram.com/colleen_callander
- facebook.com/Colleen-Callander
- linkedin.com/in/colleen-callander

We hope you enjoy reading this book. We'd love you to post a review on social media or your favourite bookseller site. Please include the hashtag #majorstreetpublishing.

Major Street Publishing specialises in business, leadership, personal finance and motivational non-fiction books. If you'd like to receive regular updates about new Major Street books, email info@majorstreet.com.au and ask to be added to our mailing list.

Visit majorstreet.com.au to find out more about our books and authors.

We'd love you to follow us on social media.

in linkedin.com/company/major-street-publishing

f facebook.com/MajorStreetPublishing

○ instagram.com/majorstreetpublishing

y @MajorStreetPub